THE
DREAM
TEAM

RONALD WILSON

WESTBOW
PRESS
A DIVISION OF THOMAS NELSON

ISBN: 978-1-4497-6273-5 (sc)
ISBN: 978-1-4497-6274-2 (e)
ISBN: 978-1-4497-6275-9 (hc)

Library of Congress Control Number: 2012914702

WestBow Press books may be ordered through booksellers or by contacting:

Scripture taken from the King James Version of the Bible.

Scripture quotations taken from the Holy Bible, New Living Translation, copyright 1996, 2004. Used by permission of Tyndale House Publishers, Inc., Wheaton, Illinois 60189. All rights reserved.

Scripture quotations taken from the New American Standard Bible®, Copyright © 1960, 1962, 1963, 1968, 1971, 1972, 1973, 1975, 1977, 1995 by The Lockman Foundation. Used by permission." (www.Lockman.org)

Scripture taken from the Holy Bible, New International Version®. Copyright © 1973, 1978, 1984 Biblica. Used by permission of Zondervan. All rights reserved.

Scripture taken from the Amplified Bible, Copyright © 1954, 1958, 1962, 1964, 1965, 1987 by The Lockman Foundation. Used by permission.

Scripture quotations are from The Holy Bible, English Standard Version® (ESV®), copyright © 2001 by Crossway, a publishing ministry of Good News Publishers. Used by permission. All rights reserved.

WestBow Press
A Division of Thomas Nelson
1663 Liberty Drive
Bloomington, IN 47403
www.westbowpress.com
1-(866) 928-1240

Any people depicted in stock imagery provided by Thinkstock are models, and such images are being used for illustrative purposes only.
Certain stock imagery © Thinkstock.

Printed in the United States of America

WestBow Press rev. date: 09/24/2012

The Dream Team is a God inspired book that will electrify your soul from the first page. It challenges us to look @ our company from a broader point of view. Pastor Wilson has out did himself on this one, lead by the spirit of God. I am sure all that read this book will be blessed beyond their dreams. I encourage every reader of (The Dream Team) to allow this heartfelt writing from Pastor Ronald Wilson to move you into another phase of destiny, as he is lead by the Holy Spirit to bless your soul.

-Mr. Herbert (Holy Boy) Woods
National/Int'l Recording Artist

The Dream Team: If you are looking for a way to engage with a new life perspective, this book will challenge every fiber in your thought pattern. It urges you to excel beyond your normal way of thinking. This is more than a book!!!! Follow the signs in this new and riveting message that will lead you to an extraordinary journey that awaits you ahead. Through all of the hurt, pain, disappointments and betrayal that mankind encounter in our walk with Christ, it is amazing how God can still use all of these things to produce our personal dream team. Get ready for an unprecedented word!

-Rachel Wilson
National Recording Artist & Co-Pastor
New Life Worship Center - Greensboro, N.C

When I think of The Dream Team and the power broker Ronald Wilson, I think of God using this young man's journey to let us all know that God has a Dream Team to insure us all the victory.

-Carnell Murrell
Producer/Songwriter

I have read many books but this is by far one of the most inspiring books I've examined in a while. I believe that you will find, as I have, that Pastor Wilson is a prolific writer. He also harnesses an uncanny ability to capture in written words what every individual can witness the spirit of God saying to them. Each chapter from the first to the last is riddled with gold nuggets that will leave you rich in knowledge. It is so packed with wisdom that you and everyone around you who follow the principles he reveals cannot help but become better.

I encourage you to get comfortable because when you begin reading it you will not want to put it down till you have finished.

-Elder David Reid
Elder & Distant Overseer
Church of God Apostolic, Inc.

FOREWORD

Hope, Desires: DREAMS

*"Hope deferred maketh the heart sick: but when
the desire cometh, it is a tree of life."*
Proverbs 13:12

Because man is a spirit, created in the image and after the likeness of God his Creator, there are certain attributes of God that can be found residually in all mankind. One of those attributes is the capacity to conceive of a positive difference from the present, and to perceive a future characterized by something "better". This capacity is innate to humanity; however, through the Fall, what was innate in the Creation became twisted through sin. As a result, some people's ability to conceive / perceive / believe "the better" has been damaged. Add to that the numerous ideologies that exist which condition people NOT to conceive of a positive difference in the future, their future. These ideas have been fostered through sexism, racism, classism, poverty, war, illiteracy, religiosity, and other kinds of oppression: they teach men and women not to hope, not to desire, not to aspire. The individual and collective hearts of millions have been sickened as tragically, throughout history, these ideological "assassins" have been widely, wildly successful.

But God... He does His best work in people, and for people, against the odds. And though abuses and oppressors have strangled hope and desire out of many --- leaving them zombie-like wanderers who merely exist from coincidence to fatality to statistic --- GOD shows up and gives people a "hope-and-desire package", a virtual "tree of life" called a DREAM.

A dream… that's what Jacob had --- that's what his son Joseph had --- that's what Joseph the adoptive father of Jesus had. A dream… that's what Martin Luther King Jr. had. Sometimes a dream can be a literal subliminal experience within the subconscious that occurs while one is asleep. However, a dream may also be a conscious determination driven by a passionate conviction that things can be, should be, and shall be, better. That determination is an inner PICTURE of a better world, a better nation, a better business, a better family, a better life. That picture is generally referred to as a dream. And if the dream, the desire, is from God, then the dreamer's role IN the dream will always be to help to make the better, greater thing, a reality. And if the dream is from God, the benefit of the better is not for the dreamer – it is ALWAYS BIGGER than what the dreamer himself or herself could possibly encompass. Be clear: God gives no self-serving dreams.

But if you have a hope, a desire that is bigger than you, blessing others and not just you, you should continue reading, for what Pastor Ronald Wilson shares will encourage and challenge your thoughts and your perspective of your dream. It will help you to locate where you are on your journey toward the dream's fulfillment, and it will reassure you that as lonely as the journey may seem, you are not alone. Pastor Wilson himself is a dreamer: it is his desire to impact men and women for God, to rescue the wandering and to help them to ascertain awareness of divine purpose and destiny. Join him on the journey to your life dream's fulfillment having this great assurance:

"Delight thyself also in the LORD: and he shall
give thee the desires of thine heart."
Psalm 37:4

-Michael A. Blue, Pastor
The Door of Hope Christian Church
Marion, South Carolina

CONTENTS

DEDICATION

THIS WRITING IS DEDICATED TO every believer across the globe. Its purpose is to be used as a tool to help affirm the God inspired dream you feel within the heart of your spirit. To also play a part in ushering you into a broader perspective of the people God allows you to be surrounded by on this journey called life. It can quickly become frustrating if we have a narrow perspective concerning those whom God has designed to help us reach our dreams in life.

We dedicate this writing to the leader God has called you to be as well as the present leader that you are. Sometimes we are capable of questioning the fact of the cause of people flowing in and out of our lives. God is a strategist and he will never make a mistake. There is none good but God, and he only desire good for all humankind. We cannot separate good from God so we must trust that whatever he permit in our lives, it has to be for our good. There is a purpose of the "current flow" of people in your life today. Upon reading, we pray the material shared will help broaden your perspective and purpose of life.

ACKNOWLEDGEMENTS

I MUST START BY ACKNOWLEDGING MY wife, Rachel for sacrificing and allowing me the countless hours it took me to accomplish this assignment. You understood the mandate upon this assignment and allowed me the space to birth out this writing to the world. In the challenging seasons of this writing you were always there to push me and inspire me to finish. There are not enough words I can write to thank you for your prayers and support. May God richly bless you and all that you put your hands to do!

To my sons Ronald and Gabriel, thank you for being an inspiration to me. Every time I look at you I receive a fresh breath of air that empowers me with the strength and courage I need to press on. You will never begin to imagine the major role you played in keeping me focused while tackling this assignment. You also sacrificed family time and although you may have not understood, you yet allowed me the time I was in need of to write. To my son Day'quan and my daughter Ty'kia, I love you and thank God for placing you in my life. To my mother Mae, who raised me up the best she could while facing the challenges of singleness and poverty. I love you mom!

I'm grateful to the body of New Life Worship Center of Greensboro, NC. Thank you for your continual support by way of encouraging words, texts, emails, Facebook and so on. There were times that I gained strength just by looking in your eyes and seeing that you believe in me. You have to be a special group of people to be able to deal with me every Sunday and every Tuesday (LOL)! Thank you!

To my spiritual father the late Bishop John W. Barber. You stained my spirit with a deep hunger for God and you taught me by example how to believe God through tough times. Words will never be able to express the life changing impression God transferred to me through your life! To my spiritual father and mentor Bishop Michael Blue. You are a walking inspiration to me and your life constantly encourages and challenges me to walk in a spirit of excellence! Every time you open your mouth my life is transformed! Thank you sir.

Finally the greatest thanks of ALL belongs to the Bishop of my soul, my saviour and King, the Lord Jesus Christ. Without God, none of this writing would have been possible. Through your grace and wisdom was given me the ability to conceive and birth out the seed that was planted into my spirit. Praise God from whom all blessings flow. You must know that everything that has happened to you that was good, *God did it!*

"THE DREAM" AND "THE TEAM!"

I S THERE A DREAM INSIDE of you? I'm here to tell you that you will not be able to reach it alone. If God has anything to do with it, he will obligate himself to ensure the right "Team" in everyone's life for the sole purpose of reaching his or her dream(s). Everyone must have a dream and a God-given team in order to survive.

The importance of a dream:

> Where there is no vision, the people are unrestrained, But happy is he who keeps the law.
>
> -Proverbs 29:18

The point is quit simple. In every place that a dream is not found, there is chaos. This is what's happening in our young people all over the nations. No one has trained them to dream. Now they are wild and unrestrained with no goals, no plans, and without structure. In a visionless society, anything goes! If you took the dream(s) out of every heart in the world, no one would be safe, due to the violence of all restraints that have been removed. Believe it or not, it's a dream that settles (restrains) a man. The definition of unrestrained is, not controlled or held in check. So the reality of the matter is this; a nation or individual that doesn't own a vision will be unrestrained and uncontrollable.

A man that is able to do what he wants to do whenever he wants to do it is a dangerous man. We all need a level of restraint (control) in our lives so that there will be a balance in the world. Vision brings balance and control to all humanity. I have heard people blame Satan for taking material things from them that absolutely will not benefit him. If Satan can take any one thing from a man, it would be his vision (dream). Satan knows that a man is only as strong as his dreams. We start as little children with big dreams but as we grow older, the enemy goes on the prowl and began robbing Gods people year after year. When we become grown adults, our dreams are not as broad or colorful as they were when we were children. In most cases, Satan chips off pieces of our dreams as we are growing up. About the time that we are adults, we don't own any vision at all! This is a sure sign that having a dream is at the top of the line for success to take its course in our lives.

> I had fainted, unless I had believed to see the goodness of the LORD in the land of the living.
>
> -Psalm 27:13

David is trying to get across to the reader, the reason he didn't faint when things became overwhelming was because of the dream he held in his heart. That's right, the dream held him up when all opposition was trying to take him down! He refused to let anyone, including Satan, rob him of the vision God placed in his heart. David is saying if he wouldn't have dreamed (visualized) to see Gods goodness while he was amongst the living, chances are he would not have made it. In other words, the dream kept him alive. I'm a witness to this fact. I'm sure someone can attest to the fact that they have been faced with the temptation to quit but their dream wouldn't allow them to. When you hear the voice of your outward circumstances constantly running in your head, its good to have an inward voice of your dream(s) running in your heart!

And he dreamed yet another dream, and told it his brethren, and said, Behold, I have dreamed a dream more; and, behold, the sun and the moon and the eleven stars made obeisance to me.

-Genesis 37:9

Deep within the heart of a young lad named Joseph was a dream that was planted by God. This dream caused a lot of chaos in the family but ended up saving the family. In most cases, the dream that you are housing is not really for you. This is why it is important to embody a dream because you never know the countless lives that are connected to the dream(s) God birth in your heart. If God has anything to do with it, your dream will be far too big for you to enjoy all to yourself. I know at first you may feel your dream will only be for you, but you will eventually find out that God is too big to give out a dream that will only benefit one person. I believe at first Joseph thought his dream would only benefit himself but in the end he witnessed his dream thriving to become beneficial to an entire nation. God had the entire family and nation wrapped inside the dream of one lad. I wonder what, and whom God has wrapped inside of you and your dream(s). Could it be your community, your family, your fellow associates on your job or how about the entire country. Every dream that is given by God will be a conduit to help change the world. Joseph was seventeen when he received the dream and thirty when the dream received him. There are some dreams we will take ownership of now, but it will not be until later when they will take ownership of us.

Joseph encouraged his brothers by letting them know that God allowed Satan to use them, in order to preserve much people alive. They meant it for evil, but God allowed it to work for good. There is a dream inside of you that you may have not tapped into yet that is going to be responsible for preserving nations.

PREFACE

To all that have chose to read this book and have a dream deep down in the core of your soul, it is an absolute necessity to have a team to push you into your dream(s). The flip side is this; it may not be the team you thought you needed, or the team you may have hand picked yourself. Sometimes we can make the wrong choices when it comes to picking our circle of companions. We set ourselves up for failure when we don't allow God to order our steps in life. God knows exactly who, and what we need in order to go to the next phase of our life. Scripture clearly states in Job 23:10, **"But he knoweth the way that I take..."** There is not a road in life that the finger of God will point you down, and cease his hand to provide. In other words, if God points you in a direction, his provision has already been set in place! If God directs you to a place, he will always provide in that place, just as he pointed the prophet Elijah to Zarephath and told him a widow woman was already provided to sustain him. We make a mess of things when we deny Gods direction but yet expect his provision.

What God was about to do was going to be the greatest accomplishment on the earth and Jesus couldn't accomplish it alone. Jesus goes up into a mountain and prayed to God all night concerning the team he needed to pick in order for his dream to come to pass. Out of a multitude of disciples, God points out to Jesus that all he need is twelve. The twelve apostles represented twelve different kinds of people. You are going to have to deal with more than just the people of your kind that you grew up playing card games with. You need to know how to deal with people from all walks of life that have different agendas, personalities, and that are from different nations. You have to come to grips that everybody is not going to be like you. Sometimes familiarity can become our greatest stumbling block. We grow up and become familiar with one another and our surroundings and expect for it to always remain the same.

Tradition sets in our bones like a bad cold and we find ourselves wanting to only be around those of our kind. Even in church, we can't expect everyone to shout, dance, sing or worship like us. When I first came into the church, we were known to be radical, loud and sung most songs that had an upbeat tempo. This was all I knew so when I had a chance to visit elsewhere and heard slow tempo music and off beat claps, I felt like they were doomed for hell. God had to bring me into the knowledge that everyone wasn't going to clap and dance like the church I was accustomed to. There are so many sides to God that we will never come into the full understanding of.

Jesus had to choose twelve men that were all different from each other. Jesus made sure he picked a team of diverse spirits so he would be well equipped to shepherd diversities of nations. As it was for Jesus, so it is for you. The many spirits that's around you will eventually qualify you to teach, and shepherd many nations! I know you may want every body around you to act, think and respond like you, but if you want to go further in life, you need diversity. A diversified unity (Father, Son, Holy Spirit) is what's responsible for making the world. Some of us are confused because we are in the middle of a circle of people that we feel like is on our team but can't figure out why they are always tripping. The biggest dream you could ever imagine is getting ready to come to pass because of all the diverse spirits that operate through the people that are in your life.

I'm here to tell you, all you need is twelve to reach your dream! In Jesus three years of ministry, other than the cross, the team that he chose was the most important thing he ever did! Reason being is because if it weren't for the team he picked, he would have never made it to the cross. Everybody around you, whether they are for you, or against you is on your team. It was his team that ushered him to the cross! If it wasn't for the team that he picked, the dream would have never came to pass. Jesus work extended from the time he walked the earth even until this day because of the team he chose. Truth be told, we all are here because of Jesus dream team. We will never make it to our personal cross if we don't have the correct team to push us there.

Just as Jesus, we all need a dream team that will cause our ministries to broaden and extend. While doing the work of God, it will help you to know that the work of God is like an orchestra. In an orchestra, diverse kinds of instruments are necessary to make it a success. Although they are all different, and they all release a different sound, when they play in harmony, the outcome is amazing! All kinds of different spirits in your life, all playing at the same time, (betrayal, doubt, jealousy, etc.) is going to work for you in the end and release a sound that's mighty sweet. We must allow God to place people in our life that will walk amongst us to get us where we need to be. I know you may not like everybody that's around you, but there are people around you for the sole purpose of helping birth your dream.

People come and people go, and it plays with your mentor to think something is wrong with you as an individual. I want you to know it's a strategy move by God on your behalf. God sits in your life as if he is playing a chess game. He examines the board and only makes the moves that will assure you the victory. Please know that everyone that comes in your life is not supposed to stay forever. Even after you gave them money, you paid their rent, you paid their lights, you gave them food, and some still walked out and failed to even say thank you. I don't care what you do; everybody is not going to stay. Of course they are going to leave you, they left Jesus and none of us are in the place of his faithfulness to humankind. The only one who is ordained to stay in your life forever is God! People are so fickle, and will leave you in a minute without a cause or explanation, but God will turn it around and cause it to work for your good!

Whether you know it or not, there will always be twelve different spirits constantly in rotation around you. Out of the twelve, you will need five starters. These starting players include (but are not limited to), love, boldness, denial, doubt, and betrayal. Other teammates will come in your life off the bench to play other necessary roles such as nonsupport, gazing, spectating, hating, debating and so on. Later on, there will be free agents that will be maneuvered through the leading of the lord to be a part of your team. God will always make sure he allow your life to cross paths with all those that are necessary team players that will assist in bringing your dream into fruition. God allowed Ruth to meet Naomi, Timothy to meet Paul, Elisha to cross paths with Elijah, and of course Judas to match up with Jesus. On the movie Cast Away, Tom had Wilson, Gilligan had Skipper, and Robin had Batman. I think you get the point by now. I don't care if you lived underground, if God had to run your team to you through a pipeline, that's what he will do! Whatever the case may be, you should began to bless the lord for every spirit that is working on your behalf and that is playing a part of birthing your dream!

INTRODUCTION

F ROM MY PERSPECTIVE, THE YEAR 1992 will be remembered forever. For me, 1992 is the year my eyes were opened to the reality of life. I found myself in trouble with the law, I graduated high school, I had a scare with a drug overdose, and I also was invited to a life changing revival that I'm still reaping the benefits of this very day. I'm a big sports fan, and 1992 was also the year that the Olympics opened their doors to professional basketball players.

Team USA had so many star players on their team; the only name that was worthy of housing these players was the "Dream Team". In other words, it was so unbelievable, the only way you could have a team of this magnitude was in your dreams. The team consisted of twelve of the greatest NBA stars the league has ever witnessed on the court. Larry Bird, Earvin "Magic" Johnson, Clyde "The Glide" Drexler, Chris Mullin, John Stockton, Scottie Pippen, Patrick Ewing, Christian Laettner, Charles Barkley, David Robinson, Karl Malone, and the greatest of all time, Michael Jordan. Chuck Daly, one of the greatest coaches of all time, was in the center of this unprecedented team as head coach.

The competition that faced Team USA was matchless. Every time the Dream Team stepped onto the court, they breezed their way pass every team with flying colors. 20, 30, and 40-point wins were counted to their credit. Of course team USA, brought home the gold medal, and many priceless moments on the court that will be remembered forever!

Although 1992 USA team was remarkable, and went down in history, there was a team that was put together over 2000 years prior of the dream team of twelve men who made up the original dream team. God sent his only begotten son upon the earth with a *"Dream"* in his heart to redeem the world back to himself through him. The only problem was, just as Chuck Daly had to pick a team; Jesus had to pick a team as well. A team that would help bring his dream to pass. Jesus went on to pick twelve men whose names were Simon, (whom he also named Peter), and Andrew his brother, James and John, Philip and Bartholomew, Matthew and Thomas, James the son of Alphaeus and Simon called Zelotes and Judas the brother of James and Judas Iscariot, which also was the traitor. The funny part about it was, he didn't pick perfect people. He knew he would need twelve different personalities, twelve different perspectives, twelve different spirits, twelve different opinions and so on. I once heard a man of God preach, "all you need is twelve!" I believe in my prayers, but I certainly believe in the prayers of Jesus. The bible clearly allows us to see that Jesus carefully picked this team after an all night conversation with God.

And it came to pass in those days, that he went out into a mountain to pray, and continued all night in prayer to God. And when it was day, he called unto him his disciples: and of them he chose twelve, whom also he named apostles; Simon, (whom he also named Peter,) and Andrew his brother, James and John, Philip and Bartholomew, Matthew and Thomas, James the son of Alphaeus, and Simon called Zelotes, 16 And Judas the brother of James, and Judas Iscariot, which also was the traitor.

-Luke 6:12-16

Although many criticize and preach against the twelve that were chosen, Jesus knew he had to have this imperfect team in order for "The Dream" to come to pass. Every single one played their role just as Jesus intended them to play it. Please remember, Jesus spent all night in prayer on the decision he had to make, and God gave him the team he needed to make it to the cross! Down to the starting line-up. Thank God he chose who he did because if he didn't, there is no telling where you and I would be today.

As we make an attempt to journey through this writing, it is our goal to encourage every one that is housing a dream in their spirit to read this writing and get an understanding of the importance of allowing God to pick their team. Again, the funny part will be whom God choses to stay in your life that you have tried to pray out. Believe me, I would prefer everyone that surrounds me to believe in me, love and support me as well, but sometimes that's not the team it will take to birth the dream out of you that God has placed in your heart. Remember it's not about you, but the dream that's inside of you!

CHAPTER ONE

Love

(John)

Though I speak with the tongues of men and of angels, and have not charity, I am become as sounding brass, or a tinkling cymbal. And though I have the gift of prophecy, and understand all mysteries, and all knowledge; and though I have all faith, so that I could remove mountains, and have not charity, I am nothing. And though I bestow all my goods to feed the poor, and though I give my body to be burned, and have not charity, it profiteth me nothing.

Charity suffereth long, and is kind; charity envieth not; charity vaunteth not itself, is not puffed up, Doth not behave itself unseemly, seeketh not her own, is not easily provoked, thinketh no evil; Rejoiceth not in iniquity, but rejoiceth in the truth; Beareth all things, believeth all things, hopeth all things, endureth all things.

Charity never faileth: but whether there be prophecies, they shall fail; whether there be tongues, they shall cease; whether there be knowledge, it shall vanish away. For we know in part, and we prophesy in part. But when that which is perfect is come, then that which is in part shall be done away. When I was a child, I spake as a child, I understood as a child, I thought as a child: but when I became a man, I put away childish things. For now we see through a glass, darkly; but then face to face: now I know in part; but then shall I know even as also I am known. And now abideth faith, hope, charity, these three; but the greatest of these is charity.

-I Corinthians 13:1-13

WE WILL BEGAN TO TAKE you on a quest of bringing you into a greater knowledge concerning the people God has surrounded you with to see to it that your dream(s) come to pass. Out of all the characters and players that will be positioned on your team, love is the greatest of all! Without love in life's equation there is no profit.

For the millions of battles love has been through, it has never lost one. The word of God lets us know that love never fails. From the worst-case scenario you can bring to mind, to the smallest matter in life, love is the answer. If we took love out of every equation, the answer would be chaos! Although it may be hard to recognize, *love* holds the world together! Love stands faithful after every war, every test, every circumstance, and even after every death. When everything else falls, love will still be standing!

John went down in history with the reputation as the disciple whom Jesus loved. Many will argue this point to be true for the simple reason of John being the disciple who spent the most time with Jesus, and stayed closest to him and, on many occasions was found laying upon his breast. It has always been God's will that every human being is impacted, and infected by the spirit and the power of love. Without love, we can't make it. The word of God reveals to us that God is love. So putting it in another format, we can't make it without God! God (love) is the source that's holding it all together. Without love (God) this world would fall apart. As we look into the accounts wherein God (love) was not welcomed or kicked out, catastrophe took its course. Starting from elementary schools to college campuses. Even from the courthouse to the average personal house. Also from our work place all the way down to our worship place. It doesn't matter of the "place", if God (love) is not welcome, the end will be a calamity!

Divine Love

We see our young people chasing after everything they could to try to fill voids and emptiness that only divine love is capable of filling. They join gangs; they run after sex, whether it's heterosexual, homosexual, or bisexual. They rebel and run away from home to live in the streets as beggars, drug dealers, as well as drug users. They find themselves driven, but to all the wrong liveliness. The substance we lack in our life that drives us to pursue after other temporary satisfaction is *divine love*. That's right, divine love, or love proceeding directly from God. No greater love than this, that flows from our Lord.

Although it manifests itself in abundance around us daily, we lack it because we don't recognize it, or we recognize it and simply refuse to receive it. Divine love isn't recognized because it's in the wind that blows through the trees. It's in the sand on every beach that caresses our feet with warmth as we stroll the summer shore. Divine love is in the rays of the sun and the seasons that change. This love has the knowledge to give the Eskimo as well as the polar bear and other animals the cold temperatures they need in order to live comfortably and survive. At the same time, divine love gives a totally different climate to those in need of it that are completely on the other side of the world.

Divine love will never miss, because divine love is God! The devil longs for us to chase the lesser at the same time God longs for us to own the greater! The divine love of God is far greater than any experience mankind will ever encounter. Many neglect to receive Gods love because they feel they will fail God in the walk he requires of them. Regardless of how we mentally disqualify ourselves, divine love will always have open arms for the sake of mankind to rest!

Sensual Love

Many are victims of sensual love and don't even know it. Sensual love is love that operates from the head and not the heart. It's also love that operates from our senses and not our spirits. The pleasures of mankind in its fleshly nature are driven by his senses. However our pleasures tends to change from season to season. So when the season of our pleasure changes, the way I treat you also changes. Divine love doesn't need pleasure in the middle of it to keep operating as do sensual love. Divine love operates with or without pleasure.

In sensual love, as soon as the gifts and the sex run out, you're out! Sensual love is love that exists from what I can see, taste, touch, smell and hear. In other words some believe they are in love because they can see the car their boyfriend or husband bought them or smell the roses and taste the chocolate. My friend, after the chocolate runs out and the car breaks down, its only divine love that continues to operate. Divine love will leave the ninety-nine and pursue after the lost one. Sensual love has the tendency to turn into a frozen tundra in a moment of time. Jesus stated, "the love of many shall wax cold." Our teenagers are constant victims of sensual love. They suffer so many broken hearts in their teen life, when they do get married, they are already burnt out and no good for their spouse. This is one reason the divorce rate is so high. Sensual love is a mere reflection of love divine.

Mishandled Love

I'm going to assume we are all familiar with the game hot potato. The object of the game is to toss a potato or potato-like object around and not be the one caught holding it when the buzzer goes off. As a kid I carefully observed how this object was tossed around the room or circle of people. The potato was dropped, kicked, squeezed, and mishandled in every way. I look at what we call love in the same way as this potato.

The purpose of love is not to be tossed around in the circles of life that we create. We love God, our spouse, our children, and sometimes we even love our pastors. However all of the above mention are tossed in and out of our lives based on how we are feeling in that season of our life. Love is not a hot potato, however it is often mishandled. We must be careful when we are handling someone's feelings. The divorce rate is falling off the charts and not many people are loyal to any kind of commitment. Church members are not committed to their church just as people are not committed to their jobs, spouses, and even God. We should aim to handle love as God intended us to handle life itself. Very careful!

Rebellious Love

One evening I was in the grocery store and saw a couple that challenged my thinking. There were two teenagers that were dressed in all black. Their fingernails were black, and they had piercings in every place possible. It appeared as though they were rebellious runaways. They were hugging one another as well as kissing and laughing. The appearance of love was all over them. Suddenly I heard, "rebellious love." Both of them were in love but the foundation of their love was rebellion. There are countless people in their local church that are rebellious to authority and claim to love their church. Chances are you will fall out with your church if rebellion is the driving force behind your love.

Satan was the first rebel and his *love* for control caused him to fall. The foundation of Lucifer's love was total rebellion. This rebellious love caused him and a third of heaven's angels to fall. Is love really here to fall into or to grow into? We witness people fall in and out of love on a daily basis. The question is, what was the foundation of that love they once felt. If the foundation isn't right, the house will not survive!

Prayer

> And he spoke a parable unto them to this end, that men ought always to pray, and not to faint
>
> -Luke 18:1

Prayer is a "Master Key" that will be used in our lives to usher all those whom we need into our life to help assist us in reaching our dream(s). As we previously learned, before Jesus was given a team, he went up into a mountain and prayed all night. If Jesus had to pray to be surrounded by the right team, of course we are going to have to pray. Today prayer is a rare language that's used in life today. That's right, prayer is a language. A body of words that are used to change any circumstance life is capable of bringing our way. The sad truth is prayer is also rare for those who are known as "believers".

Before there is revival there must be prayer. Before there is healing, reconciliation, spiritual growth and understanding, prayer must be pursued. Every major revival that has ever hit a nation was ushered in by way of prayer. Gods' people are continually being robbed of what's rightfully theirs because of the lack of prayer. Prayer invites God to enter into mans' domain and gives his will the liberty it needs to be done on earth "as" it is done in heaven. If you are expecting any move of God in your life it will be to your benefit to precede that move with prayer. Jesus teaches that men (mankind) ought to always pray and not faint.

God's choice

As we closely examine the ministry of Jesus, we see that he surrounded himself with twelve men who all had different values, personalities and backgrounds. Many question the wisdom of the Lord and his choosing. I've heard some ask "If God knew everything why would he choose people to follow him that will later, betray, deny, challenge him and question him? I have come to the defense of God, to assure all, that God is indeed omniscience. God has the capacity to know everything infinitely, and has maximal knowledge to understand and perceive all things. That's the sole reason why God chose whom he did to surround him. Every event was imminent in Christ's life in order for his dream to come to pass. So with no mistakes and no regrets, Jesus picks a dream team that would help him change the world.

Have you ever wondered why certain people were in your life that you knew really didn't have your best interest at heart. You saw betrayal, and that they really didn't believe in you. They also renege on supporting you, however God allows them to stay around in your life even after you tried to pray them out. This may be hard to intake, but what if I told you God purposely allowed those headaches to stay in your life because they had their rightful place on your dream team. The entire time you may have viewed them as hurting you, but God views them as helping you.

It's challenging to understand what God has for you in the long run. For where God has planned and positioned your future, you can't get there by a regular launching pad. Believe me, it's the irregular circumstances that's going to launch you into places you have never imagined! It is my assignment to help unfold a broader perspective of those whom God allows you to come in contact with as you pursue your God given dream. The team you want may not be the team you need! What better player to start off with than John (Love).

Our Forerunner

> For God so loved the world, that he gave his only begotten Son, that whosoever believeth in him should not perish, but have everlasting life.
>
> -John 3:16

Before there were offering lines in any church setting, there was one in heaven. God stood as the forerunner of the principle of giving, and *gave* his only begotten son. When it comes to giving, no one can out-give God! From day one, and prior, God has always been found giving. He gave the world its form, and pattern. He gave all animals and humankind life and purpose. He gives us joy, peace, new mercy every morning and the list never stops. God is the giver of all life. He was our perfect prototype model in the field of giving. The reason why he is able to give so much is because he love so much.

Love places all humankind in position to be able to give. Show me a person that doesn't give much and I will show you a person who doesn't love much. God was able to give because he first loved. Whenever love is in our lives, it places us in position to give. Love prompts us to give our best efforts, give our best seed, gifts, etc. The power of love is constantly underestimated but without it, there will be no power to *give*. Can you imagine what kind of world it would be without us being able to give? It would be a miserable world with no love and no meaning.

> He that loveth not knoweth not God; for God is love.
>
> -1 John 4:8

Tree examination

Even so every good tree bringeth forth good fruit; but a corrupt tree bringeth forth evil fruit. A good tree cannot bring forth evil fruit, neither can a corrupt tree bring forth good fruit. Every tree that bringeth not forth good fruit is hewn down, and cast into the fire. Wherefore by their fruits ye shall know them.

-Matthew 7:17-20

The fruit of an individual that knows the Lord is the love that egress from that individual. John loved his leader (Jesus) and it showed continually. Scripture tells us that God is love, so everything found outside of love is outside of God. We must be careful in life not to be found walking in the spirit of error. Everything outside of the word of the Lord is error. God doesn't want his people walking in hatred, but in love.

The easiest way to recognize a tree is by its fruit. Apple trees produce apples. Pear trees produce pears, and love is the bi-product of a tree produced of God. You can never go wrong discerning a tree if you closely observe the fruit which it bears. In order to love, one must know God. If love isn't flowing from the tree, it just may be a God-less tree. These types of trees are scary and I would warn you to be careful before you pick off of them. There was once a couple that belonged to the church my wife and I were the pastors of. This husband and wife knew that my wife and I had a well-balanced marriage. Far from perfect but very well balanced. At the time there also was a sister in the church that had been married and divorced at least four times. Of course you know what I'm about to say. The couple failed to examine the tree and its fruit. They went behind our backs to receive words of wisdom concerning their marriage from Sister Doe. To make a long story short, they ate the fruit of that tree and they are not married to this date. Examine the tree and God will give you the eye to discern the good from the bad.

Fruit Test

Far too long have people been tricked by wolves pretending to be sheep in the church. You would be surprised to know how many people in the church portray to be good fruit but are really corrupt to the core. Here are a few ways to test fruit to see if it's good or bad.

Test one - Check the date

With the same caution we use in a grocery store before buying fruit, we can use in our everyday life. Just as we check the date on milk, eggs, and fruit in the grocery store, we can use this same technique in our church to bring us into a greater knowledge of the people around us. By checking the date I mean, when was the last time they apologized first? When was the last time they acted the role of a peacemaker? Is there walk with Christ up-to-date, or are they yet living off memories of good deeds in their past? When we check the dates on products in the store and they are out of date, what do we do? The answer is, we put it back on the shelf. We don't buy it! When someone is acting to be one thing but the date is saying another thing, don't buy it! You don't have to buy into someone that you know is not good fruit.

Test two- Squeeze Test

The squeeze test is the test of pressure. Before buying most fruit, you should apply a small bit of pressure to it to see if its contents are firm. You don't want to take home fruit that appear to be firm, only to find out its mushy and rotten inside later. After applying pressure, that fruit should be able to bounce back to its original state.

Some people are ultra-sensitive and can't handle any pressure. The slightest thing you say or do offend them. They can't handle any kind of transition with ministry or leadership. Every time they are squeezed, they burst and find it difficult to bounce back. These are fruit (people) we should strongly consider before buying into to spare us disappointment.

Test three- Mold Test

The smallest patch of mold stores toxins that are capable of traveling through an entire fruit. Most people are tempted to cut off the mold spot and take their chances at eating the remainder of the fruit that has no visible mold. The danger lies in the invisible. We should be aware of the invisible toxins that have occupied the space of the remaining fruit

This is how some people are. They can accompany their self around a person that has mold and reap the toxins of that relationship. They may not know it, or recognize it, but the mold from their companion(s) has now corrupted their character, personality, and manners. If you see the mold, don't buy it!

Test Four- Holes

Holes are a sign that a fruit has been bitten, tampered with, or has insect infestation. Many people have holes and find it difficult to contain anything God puts in them. These holes can be a result of various things. Growing up without a father, abuse, neglect, are a few areas of concern that may lead to puncturing holes into a persons heart. There's a chance that our deepest secrets and passions will be leaked out of individuals with holes. Before you pour your thoughts into the fruit, make sure the fruit is capable of holding your information.

Test Five- Smell Test

There are some people you can be around for a short period of time and feel a bad vibe coming from them. You then know that something is not right about this person. This is exactly how the smell test is. If you pick up a fruit that smells like ammonia, you definitely shouldn't buy it. A fruit should always smell like what it is!

It's not good if you are around someone that releases a bad smell in everything they do. They release bad manners, bad habits, and bad attitudes. We must understand if we are found amongst this kind of fruit, the smell is transferable and before long the smell will spill over into our lives as well.

> But God commendeth his love toward us, in that, while we were yet sinners, Christ died for us.
>
> -Romans 5:8

True love challenges every man to esteem his neighbor more than he does himself. Another way of spelling love is *sacrifice!* It doesn't matter what you were doing, planning to do, going or planning to go, love was aimed in your direction and sacrifice saved you. Thank God for the power of love that drove Jesus to the cross and drove us away from eternal hell.

> Then Peter, turning about, seeth the disciple whom Jesus loved following; which also leaned on his breast at supper, and said, Lord, which is he that betrayeth thee?
>
> -John 21:20

In this case John was looking into the matter out of concern of the statement his master had made at supper. Love will always be concerned of all human needs. Time after time, there will be people whom God will plant in your life that will have your best interest at heart. Not that Jesus was in need of any encouragement but I believe this concern from John gave Jesus a free space in time to feel as if someone cared.

> Then she runneth, and cometh to Simon Peter, and to the other disciple, whom Jesus loved, and saith unto them, They have taken away the Lord out of the sepulchre, and we know not where they have laid him.
>
> -John 20:2

As we read some of the more prominent and familiar passages of scripture recorded on the subject of love, we must absorb the essence of love and realize we all need it. Love plays a mandatory part in a person's dream coming to pass. John was not just on the team, but he played on the starting lineup. Jesus was the essence of love, so he knew he needed to be surrounded by love in order to make it to the cross. Along the journey of life, it will be difficult to make it without someone around you that truly loves you unconditionally. 99% of the time when a teen runs away, they have a very difficult time in the streets and in some cases many of them lose total focus on all life, and unfortunately many of them lose their life. The reason behind all of this is a lack of, or no love at all. Love is what's responsible for keeping marriages together, communities thriving, and nations exalted. Proverbs 14:34 declares that "righteousness exalteth a nation: but sin is a reproach to any people." Righteousness is an offspring of love. Without love, none can be righteous. So the text is actually saying, love lifts a nation. The New Living Translation quotes, "Godliness makes a nation great, but sin is a disgrace to any people". Notice Godliness, or "Loveliness" is what's responsible for the exalting. The point I'm trying to get across to you is simply this; love is a necessity in the up building of your dream and destiny. Love encouraged Jesus to take our sin upon him that we may take his righteousness upon us. He became sin that we may become righteous (love).

For he hath made him to become sin for us, who knew no sin;
that we might be made the righteousness of God in him.

-2 Corinthians 5:21

I believe every one that has a dream inside of them is going to need a
player to start on their team in the position of love. We may compare
love to the point guard of the team. A point guard is someone who
knows how to handle the ball, keep the team focused, and help push
his team into victory. Just as a point guard knows how to handle a
ball, love knows how to handle any situation that comes in its way.
Whenever things seem to get overwhelming to the point you want
to give up, you need someone that will love you back in the game.
I believe that God obligates himself to plant at least one person in
each of our lives that will be sure that love flows around us.

This has to be true because if God doesn't plant any one in our life
that loves us, then in actuality God did not plant himself because
God is love. If we will open our hearts and receive, everyone has a
John on their team. It may not be the person you would prefer your
John to be, but we all have a John. God knew we couldn't make
it without one. For some, John may be an overlooked lad in your
community whose fashion is not up to date. Or how about that
inconspicuous niece or nephew that's in your family that thinks
the world of you. Maybe it's someone on your job that cares for you
but you really don't care much for him or her. In most cases, we are
guilty for allowing the sin of familiarity to set in even with a spouse
and you can't see that they love you. There will always be someone
on your team that loves you because God ordained love to be. The
songwriter said, "When nothing else could help, love lifted me".

The King

Love and faithfulness keep a king safe; through love his throne is made secure.

-Proverbs 20:28 (NIV)

God ordained earth as mans domain (Kingdom). Ps 115:16 lets us know that the earth belongs to man. "The heavens belong to the lord but the earth he has given to all humanity". (NLT)

As we all know, there cannot be a kingdom without a king. God has positioned mankind as kings in the earth. We also know, God is the King of Kings! Being that you are a king that reigns in the earth, you are going to need love around you to be able to stand. Yes, even a king is upheld with love. God can never fall because love never fails! As long as you have John (love) around, it's hard to be defeated.

The support from "The King", for the king

When I said, "My foot is slipping," your love, O LORD, supported me.

-Psalm 94:18 (NIV)

All kings (people) need support. The psalmist is confessing, "When I lost balance of everything and almost fell under the pressure, the only thing that braced, and supported my fall was your love. God has placed us here as kings in the earth and made sure that he allowed our lives to cross paths with someone who would support us with love.

The beginning of the word of the LORD by Hosea. And the LORD said to Hosea, Go, take unto thee a wife of whoredoms and children of whoredoms: for the land hath committed great whoredom, departing from the LORD.

-Hosea 1:2

I will go down believing the greatest love story in the bible is that of Hosea and Gomer. God knew that Gomer had a king inside of her but love was missing and the king failed to show up. As stated above in Psalm 94:18, Gomer's foot slipped time after time but God set Hosea in place to love her back into place. It didn't matter what sin Gomer committed, the love of God that flowed through her husband supported her, and kept her from falling. Gomer tried to quit but love wouldn't allow her to. It doesn't matter who you are, every man need love. Love is an essential ingredient for success in life. Open up and allow John (love) to start on your dream team. I know you may have been hurt before and think you cant love again, or be loved again. God has someone on the earth that is designed to love and support you!

Confidants

A man of many companions may come to ruin, but there is a friend who sticks closer than a brother.

-Proverbs 18:24 (NIV)

A friend loves at all times, and a brother is born for adversity.

-Proverbs 17:17 (NIV)

A confidant is one of the greatest symbols of love. They come a dime a dozen and should be greatly appreciated when they are discovered. Confidants are so scarce, when you come across one you should thank God because some people do not cross paths with a true confidant in a lifetime. Sometimes I believe we may lack the knowledge to know who our confidants are, or we know who they are but refuse to receive them due to their economic, social, or educational status. We must be careful not to allow our God connections to slip out of our life because they fail to match our personal profiles for life. Just because it's not wrapped in the paper you prefer doesn't mean the contents are not valuable. There are people who may not look like you or dress like you but they are God-ordained to help you in areas no one else can. Confidants are people who carry love in their heart for you and are not afraid of telling you the truth. When everyone else walk away, your confidants will remain.

CHAPTER 2

Betrayal

(Judas and rest of disciples).

For it was not an enemy that reproached me; then I could have borne it: neither was it he that hated me that did magnify himself against me; then I would have hid myself from him: But it was thou, a man mine equal, my guide, and mine acquaintance. We took sweet counsel together, and walked unto the house of God in company

-Psalm 55:12-14 (KJV)

GOING FROM ONE EXTREME TO the other, betrayal is the total opposite of love, but we all will experience it and we all need it to launch us into our greatest dreams. Jesus (Judas), Joseph (his brethren), David (His companions), Paul (John whose surname was Mark), Naomi (Orpah), Hosea (Gomer), Sampson (Delilah) just to name a few who were amongst many who were betrayed as we study the word of God.

Betrayal was here before any man was. As we study scripture we see that Lucifer, and a third of heaven's angels betrayed God. As we look further, God was then betrayed by creation in the Garden of

Eden. Here we see again how God was our forerunner even when it came to being betrayed. Betrayal doesn't feel good but if you love the Lord and if you are making an effort to walk out the assignment he gave you, he makes betrayal work for your good! Look at how God handled his betrayal and also look at what was birthed out of it. When Lucifer betrayed God, God handled it by going to the next plan and phase of creation. When man betrayed God, God knew how to take one righteous family and start over again.

You can't allow betrayal to cause you to just quit. You have to learn how to open a new chapter in your life and move on. The end of one thing is the beginning of another. The end of an old thing is the beginning of something new. Anytime Satan see fit to get in the heart of someone to betray you, God will also see fit to bring you through it with a mighty strong hand!

Betrayal travels deep into the core of the heart and unfortunately can become devastating if its not handled properly. One must know how to handle betrayal in order to overcome it. Most victims of betrayal take it so personal that they shut down on life itself and lose all touch with the outside world, including their dreams, goals and desires.

You are not alone

Many have fell victim to the silent cry of **"I'm the only one"**. Have you ever found yourself in a situation in life where it seems like you were being picked on by the world? This is where the prophet Elijah found himself as he began to talk to God in *1 Kings 18:22*, Then Elijah said to them, **"I am the only one** of the Lords prophets left, but Baal has four hundred and fifty prophets". When you go through enough hardships in life as Elijah, sometimes they can be so devastating that they will change your entire mindset and your perspective of life.

One of Satan's primary tools in our hardships is isolation. If he could get us by ourselves and allow us to stay there, he knows he can plant this **"Only One"** mentality on us. Once we feel like this, we began to withdraw from others because we feel abnormal. This is Satan's plan that's beginning to go into action. Most suicides occur when a person is alone. The victim is challenged by the will to live or die in his or her place of isolation. Most drug and alcohol overdoses happen when a person is alone. Most pornography and food indulging happens in the midnight hour when a person is alone!

You must know that you are not alone. There are thousands and maybe millions of people that are going through the same thing you are and maybe even worst. Believe me when I tell you, you are certainly not alone when it comes to being betrayed! Lets look at some prominent names that were betrayed but in the end, betrayal worked in their favor.

> And when they saw him afar off, even before he came near unto them, they conspired against him to slay him. And they said one to another, Behold, this dreamer cometh. Come now therefore, and let us slay him, and cast him into some pit, and we will say, Some evil beast hath devoured him: and we shall see what will become of his dreams.
>
> -Genesis 37:18-20

Joseph

Innocent seventeen year old boy that fell asleep one evening and as his head hit his pillow, God placed a dream in his heart. Joseph never asked for it, God voluntarily gave it to him. No doubt, the dream was from God, but the events that would occur to bring the dream to pass was breath taking. God has a way of showing you a glimpse of your destiny but he tends to hide the in between. He transports us from glory to glory in the way he see best. The glories are awesome, but boy I can't say the same about the "to". The "to" is the process between the glories. God promised Paul he would make it to Rome but never told him about his shipwreck in Melita or the snakebite he would suffer.

What do you do when you find yourself in the middle of a paradox? This is where Joseph life was headed although he didn't know it. God showed the young kid that he would reign, but things quickly seemed to contradict the dreams Joseph experienced.

Joseph finds himself in what I would like to call "the contradiction season". After dreaming of reigning, he tastes the first sting of betrayal and find himself looking up out of a dark waterless pit that his flesh and blood were responsible for throwing him into to die. He later gets sold into slavery and was betrayed by Potiphar's wife in the palace. This betrayal leads him into prison where God uses him to interpret a dream for the butler and the baker only to be betrayed for the third time by the chief butler that forgot about Joseph once he was free. Although it may have caused the young man a lot of hurt, each betrayal ushered him closer to his dream, and eventually placed him in the position of ruler of all Egypt. If I told you that your greatest betrayal would play a major role in your greatest triumphs would you believe me? Well it's true; if you are a victim of betrayal, get ready to be a victor in a major assignment in life!

Jesus

But there are some of you that believe not. For Jesus knew from the beginning who they were that believed not, and who should betray him.

-John 6:64

It is of a surety that Jesus knew whom he chose and why he chose them. He knew that some believed, and others were still not fully persuaded in their mind. He knew exactly whom it was that believed not but he also knew they were essential for the team. As stated previously, some challenge the decision Jesus made when he chose Judas. God knew how necessary Judas would be in the plan of redeeming the world back to himself.

The world stood still and swung on the hinges of one decision. The decision was if betrayal from a man that followed, served, and was considered to be a companion of Jesus would sell him out with a kiss. Judas would play his role on the dream team just as God intended him to do. Sometimes a game that ends at the buzzer is the most thrilling. We bite our nails, we can't sit down, we pace, we cheer, the ball goes up, and we all stand and watch in awe awaiting the outcome. That's exactly what happened to this world. Satan and all of hell's angels were gathered around ready to cheer and celebrate, as Jesus would be betrayed with a kiss from one of his very own. The kiss went up, the atmosphere grew still, and the dream was about to be made manifest.

At the risk of being negative, there is a certainty of betrayal for all of us on a personal level. There's no need to fret or panic due to betrayal. Although betrayal hurts, it is one of the healthiest things that could ever happen to you. Number one, it allows you to experience the keeping power, love, and faithfulness of God. Number two; it allows you to find out your own strengths and weaknesses. You will never know what you can take until you take it!

Please know that it is impossible to be betrayed by an enemy. When you are betrayed it will always be someone who is close to you. A friend, a family member, a co-worker, or a church member, are amongst many that are suspects of your betrayal. I know it doesn't sound pleasant but it's reality. David said it wasn't his enemy that reproached him, if it was he said he could have handled it. But it was an acquaintance that served in Gods house as he did. When Judas betrayed Jesus, Jesus replied to him as "friend". If it wasn't for the betrayal of Jesus, the dream would have became a nightmare for mankind. Be encouraged and look up in the midst of your betrayal. Your dream depends upon it! When you see what God birth out of your betrayal, you too will refer to all of them as "Friend"!

Lusting Away

Temptation comes from our own desires, which entice us and drag us away.

-James 1:14 (NLT)

Far too long have people blamed leadership and others for the reason they left churches turned their back on leadership and all those whom were considered members of the church. There is a side to man that gets fulfillment in blaming others of his or her failures. If a person is not careful, they will allow their lusts to cause them to walk away and betray people that really care for and love them. The only problem, lust is a very selfish spirit and it will drive an individual to forget about everyone else's feelings as long as their fleshly desires are fulfilled. The only reason for pulling up their stakes and departing out of your life is due to their own lust. Their conscious beats on them every time they are in your presence because of where they have allowed their lust to drive them. They know they cannot continue to face you as a man or woman of God so they would rather make up an excuse of why they walked out of your church or turned their back on you as a friend.

I will never be able to understand how a person can just get up and leave without a cause or any kind of explanation. They leave and expect everyone else to figure out why. They are not man or woman enough to tell you the truth about their struggle so they take it upon themselves and just leave. Leaving is not the problem but how they leave is the problem. People either don't know the full interpretation of them leaving, or they do know and just don't care. You must understand when you leave a church you walk out on everyone that's connected to that church. When most people turn away from a ministry, they turn away from everything connected to that ministry. Lust is a bad way to cause someone to walk out another person life but it happens all the time. In these times, God will supply the grace we need to make it through.

The Kiss

> Rise up, let us go; lo, he that betrayeth me is at hand. And immediately, while he yet spake, cometh Judas, one of the twelve, and with him a great multitude with swords and staves, from the chief priests and the scribes and the elders. And he that betrayed him had given them a token, saying, Whomsoever I shall kiss, that same is he; take him, and lead him away safely. And as soon as he was come, he goeth straightway to him, and saith, Master, master; and kissed him. And they laid their hands on him, and took him.
>
> -Mark 14:42-46

At some point in your life you will experience a kiss of betrayal from a few close players. Remember, you can only be betrayed by someone close to you. Even though it may hurt and leave you startled, that kiss will be one of the greatest things that will ever happen in your life. A kiss is a sign of love and affection so how could someone kiss you and then walk out of your life. Well, let me remind you of Orpah. After all she went through following alongside of Naomi, she ended their relationship with a kiss. She witnessed the personal struggle of her sister-in-law Ruth, as well as her mother-in-law Naomi. During the time that Naomi was in the most need of companionship,

Orpah kissed her and walked away, never to return. I don't know the reason why but this is how it usually goes; in the time you need someone the most, that's the time betrayal take its course.

In the case with Jesus and with Naomi, **"The Kiss"** was the greatest thing that happened to both of them. A kiss led Jesus to the cross, which then led you and me into salvation. Naomi's kiss led Ruth into reaping the field and finding her Boaz. Brace yourself and know that God will cause your bad to work for your good!

David

> And it came to pass on the morrow, that the evil spirit from God came upon Saul, and he prophesied in the midst of the house: and David played with his hand, as at other times: and there was a javelin in Saul's hand. And Saul cast the javelin; for he said, I will smite David even to the wall with it. And David avoided out of his presence twice.
>
> -1 Samuel 18:10-11

There isn't any hurt that exists that can take the place of the hurt of being betrayed by those in leadership. All David wanted to be was a son but even in his pure desires, the enemy had other plans towards David. David was promoted into the house of Saul and started serving as soon as he entered into Saul's life. In the seasons of Saul's heaviness, David ministered to his leader Saul for times of refreshing will be ushered into his life. There are times that you will strive to do your best to help those whom God has placed in your life as leaders but even with doing your best, there are times when things may turn sour. If leadership is not strong and solid, they can be threatened and intimidated by the victories and accomplishments of those who follow them.

It's going to work for your good!

And we know that all things work together for good to them
that love God, to them who are the called according to his
purpose.

-Romans 8:28

When I first came into the church and began studying Gods word,
I had a very shallow understanding of scripture. I'm assuming I
did like a lot of others. I opened the bible and sometimes I started
reading in the middle or the end of a chapter. There isn't anything
wrong with this technique but we must be careful and consider the
danger of it. The danger of this is taking a verse and using it out of
context with the entire chapter.

Paul guarantees that all things will work for the good, number
one "to them that love the Lord". You know just as well as I do,
everybody do not love the Lord. Number two, " to them that are the
called *according to his (GODS) purpose*". God has a set assignment
(purpose) for your life and to all that will strive to fulfill it, God will
make sure all things will work for your good.

This is good to know because betrayal is not a good thing but God
will cause it to work for your good. As stated above, an enemy can't
betray you. Only those who are close to you have the ability to betray
you. This is why betrayal hurts so badly because it comes from those
dearest to you. Any one that God allowed to walk out of your life,
God knew you didn't need them but for the short season they were
with you. God saw that their season was up with you and they
may have caused you more harm in the future, even to the point of
forfeiting your destiny!

Selfishness

> Do nothing out of selfish ambition or vain conceit. Rather, in
> humility value others above yourselves, 4 not looking to your
> own interests but each of you to the interests of the others.
>
> -Philippians 2:3-4(NIV)

You can link selfishness in most cases of betrayal. People are so self-centered they will seek out every way to appease their self and leave you when they are not getting anything out of it. Judas got money for betraying Jesus, Orpah regained idol living for betraying Naomi, Gomer's reason for betraying Hosea was her self-satisfying harlot lifestyle, and the list continues. If someone betrayed you, you owe God praise for two reasons. One is you didn't need anyone in your life that was so full of self to the point they turned their back on you. Second, God moved them out of your life after their assignment was complete and God will use their betrayal to work for good in your life.

For the sake of drugs, selfishness will cause a drug addict to take the life of a hard working mother or father to fulfill a temporary void in their life. For a moment of joy, hoarders buy items for self pleasure but eventually suffer from being overcrowded in their home and in their lives in general. Everything Jesus did in his three years of ministry was for the purpose of others. We must arm ourselves likewise and put forth an effort to support the dreams of others. We all are going to face struggles in our life, but in your time of struggle don't allow selfishness to turn you away from those who love you.

CHAPTER 3

Boldness

(Peter)

For God hath not given us the spirit of fear; but of power, and of love, and of a sound mind.

-2 Timothy 1:7

IT HAS NEVER BEEN GODS will that humankind should fear. Fear is the devil's toy that keeps a lot of Gods children from pursuing after their dreams. When we don't pursue, we are held captive within the enemy's playground. God has always intended for us to go forward in life and posses everything God has ever promised. We must be bold and also be accompanied with at least one person that is as bold as we are.

If God didn't give us the spirit of fear, then who did? Satan of course! What a gift to hand out to as many people that will receive. Sad to say, most people have accepted this gift from Satan and rejected Gods gift of power, love, and that of a sound mind. Your destiny awaits you, however it cannot be entered into without faith and boldness!

The wicked flee when no man pursueth: but the righteous are
bold as a lion

-Proverbs 28:1

You can't hook up with people who are always running from the
challenges of life. The scripture is allowing us to see if we partner
with wicked people, we will always be on the run from things that
are not even chasing us. We will never be able to complete any of our
earthly assignments on earth if we are always fearful or surrounded
by fearful people.

We should all have someone in our life that is bold. The scripture say
that we should be as bold as lions. A lion is the most feared creature
in the jungle, but also the one who has no fear. Fear is totally absent
from the life of the king of the jungle. The righteous is placed in
the same category. Boldness is a necessity in the kingdom of God!
Without it, you will be robbed from countless doors God intended
for you to walk through.

A Bold Choice

The term "fear not" is recorded throughout the bible. As a matter
of fact, you can find it in most books of the bible. Every great man
and woman of God was commanded by God to fear not. Abram,
Moses, Joshua, Sarah; just to name a few. God knew they all had
great destiny ahead of them and he (God) also knew that fear would
rob the great journey that was ahead of all of them. In order for us
to enter the promise, we must be strong and very courageous!

When Jesus chose his twelve Apostles, he made sure Peter (boldness)
was in the number. Jesus knew he would need someone around him
that wasn't afraid of a good challenge! You can easily quit and go

under if you don't have any one around you that will be bold enough to say "we can do it" no matter what the "It" is. Far too many times we fall victims to the limits of fearful, visionless people. Have you ever prematurely shared a dream, vision, goal, or assignment with someone close to you that you thought you could trust? As soon as you shared it, there response was "Nobody never did that in our family; everybody that tried always failed that's why I'm not even going to try" or "Are you sure you heard God?" A family member, a co-worker, maybe even some lukewarm church member have echoed these vain woes in your ear. There are several things Peter did to allow his boldness to stand out, but three of them are at the top of his list.

Number One-

"Thou Art the Christ Confession"

When Jesus came into the coasts of Caesarea Philippi, he asked his disciples, saying, Whom do men say that I the Son of man am? And they said, Some say that thou art John the Baptist: some, Elias; and others, Jeremias, or one of the prophets. He saith unto them, But whom say ye that I am? And Simon Peter answered and said, Thou art the Christ, the Son of the living God.

And Jesus answered and said unto him, Blessed art thou, Simon Barjona: for flesh and blood hath not revealed it unto thee, but my Father which is in heaven. And I say also unto thee, That thou art Peter, and upon this rock I will build my church; and the gates of hell shall not prevail against it. And I will give unto thee the keys of the kingdom of heaven: and whatsoever thou shalt bind on earth shall be bound in heaven:

and whatsoever thou shalt loose on earth shall be loosed in heaven.

Matthew 16:13-19(KJV)

Sometimes when you are outnumbered, it is challenging to step forward and allow your difference to shine. This is one of the many causes of why the world is falling apart. The absence of true leadership has placed our country in desperate need of revival. It's extremely difficult to find credible leaders in the earth today. True leadership begins in our homes but in most cases the father (God ordained leader) is missing. Our children are left with no vision or guidance from their own fathers and it leave them no other choice but to cast off restraint.

Leading can be one of the loneliest places in the world. Reason being is because when you lead, you see, hear, and receive everything differently. Without any thought or hesitation, Peter stepped forward from the rest and declared with boldness "Thou art the Christ, the son of the living God!" Regardless of what we think, it required boldness to be able to make a declaration of this magnitude in the midst of silence. Although Peter gets a lot of criticism, I like Peter. He knew how, and when to step forward. Time and time again when everyone else was waiting for something to happen, Peter had the boldness to just make it happen. You need somebody on your team that will make things happen and not wait for them to happen. Many secondary leaders and other laity will be responsible for the burnout of primary leadership in the church world today due to the lack of stepping forward to make things happen but rather sit back and wait for primary leadership to do it all! It's time to get the mind of Peter and step into your place of bold leadership!

Number Two-

"Bid Me Come"

And in the fourth watch of the night Jesus went unto them, walking on the sea. And when the disciples saw him walking on the sea, they were troubled, saying, It is a spirit; and they cried out for fear. But straightway Jesus spake unto them, saying, Be of good cheer; it is I; be not afraid. And Peter answered him and said, Lord, if it be thou, bid me come unto thee on the water. And he said, Come. And when Peter was come down out of the ship, he walked on the water, to go to Jesus.

-Matthew 14:25-29

When it seemed as though it was all over, Jesus showed himself to yet be Lord to his disciples in the most unexpected time. I'm guessing that they were all in a relaxed state of mind when all of a sudden a spirit appeared and they all thought it was a ghost. After Jesus calmed their fear and affirmed that it was him that was walking on the water, the only one that stepped forward to approach the matter was Peter. Boldness responded, "If it's you, bid me to come." Although Peter's response was personal, Jesus response was corporate. Jesus didn't say Peter come. He simply replied, "*come.*" As soon as the word went out, any one that was on the boat could have stepped out on that word. However, the only one that stepped out was Peter. Because of boldness, Peter now owns a testimony that no one else except for Jesus can testify of. Peter is now able to testify that his boldness allowed him to walk on water. Once again my friend, you need someone on your team that is not afraid to step out on something that has never been done before.

Number Three
The Striking of the Sword

When Jesus had spoken these words, he went forth with his disciples over the brook Cedron, where was a garden, into the which he entered, and his disciples. And Judas also, which betrayed him, knew the place: for Jesus ofttimes resorted thither with his disciples. Judas then, having received a band of men and officers from the chief priests and Pharisees, cometh thither with lanterns and torches and weapons.

Jesus therefore, knowing all things that should come upon him, went forth, and said unto them, Whom seek ye? They answered him, Jesus of Nazareth. Jesus saith unto them, I am he. And Judas also, which betrayed him, stood with them. As soon then as he had said unto them, I am he, they went backward, and fell to the ground. Then asked he them again, Whom seek ye? And they said, Jesus of Nazareth.

Jesus answered, I have told you that I am he: if therefore ye seek me, let these go their way: That the saying might be fulfilled, which he spake, Of them which thou gavest me have I lost none. Then Simon Peter having a sword drew it, and smote the high priest's servant, and cut off his right ear. The servant's name was Malchus.

-John 18:1-10

It may not have been the way Jesus wanted the situation to be dealt with but we must give props to Peter that at least he tried! Once again in front of everyone else, Peter was the only one bold enough to step forward to defend his leader. I don't know if Peter was the only one that had a sword in his possession, but I do know he was the only one bold enough to use it. I have been fortunate enough to cross paths with many talented people. The only problem is, I will never understand why should we own a talent if we are not going to use it. Gods' people are loaded with weapons (gifts, talents, and abilities) but it defeats the purpose to have something you never plan to use. Peter had a sword and felt that whenever opportunity allowed, he would take advantage.

Most people who never experience success are people who never took advantage of opportunity. Even though you may be wrong as Peter was, Jesus will fix it and show you your mistakes. If people who are not bold enough to try something new surround you, you may need to reexamine your team. God is ready to place companions in your life that's not afraid of a fight!

Number four-

"To whom shall we go?"

> And he said, Therefore said I unto you, that no man can come unto me, except it were given unto him of my Father. From that time many of his disciples went back, and walked no more with him. Then said Jesus unto the twelve, Will ye also go away? Then Simon Peter answered him, Lord, to whom shall we go? thou hast the words of eternal life. And we believe and are sure that thou art that Christ, the Son of the living God.
>
> -John 6:65-69

There are far too many people who feel like they know all the answers and they don't need anyone else. Have you ever ran into anyone you tried to coach or mentor and everything you were trying to tell them they would respond by saying "I know, I know", even before you finished saying what you were trying to say? You may feel as I do in those moments and respond by saying "if you know, why are you not doing what you know?" Peter knew Jesus was the Christ, and he also knew he had to live off of the words that came out of Jesus's mouth. So he postured himself, and did what he knew. This was another sign of boldness that flowed through Peter's life as he made this statement. Peter was letting Jesus know in front of everyone else that he realize he couldn't make it without the Lord.

The pride of life is the biggest silent killer that's responsible for taking out countless numbers of great men and women. Peter was saying, he knew he didn't have anywhere else to go to receive what he needed in order to survive. All he knew, and was comfortable with was Jesus. To some, all you know is "church", that's why every time you try to leave what you know, it seems as if your world begins to fall apart. Don't allow pride to have you as a statistic, make a bold statement as did Peter, and receive life!

Statement of boldness

> And Caleb stilled the people before Moses, and said, Let us go up at once, and possess it; for we are well able to overcome it.
>
> -Numbers 13:30

Caleb is definitely one you would want on your team. It didn't matter that others brought a negative report back, Caleb had to tell everyone to be quiet and confirmed to them that they were more than qualified to do whatever it took to reap the promises of God! Caleb made a bold statement and will go down in my mental library of boldness! I cannot stress it enough concerning the people that surround you on a day-to-day basis. Your circle can help you in birthing your dream(s) or help abort them.

We need people such as Caleb in our lives to stand up and rise over the fear and disbelief of others. People have a tendency to be easily influenced and in a lot of cases the negative will try to be the majority. People seem to follow the crowd, but God will always raise up someone that has the boldness to silence the crowd. Caleb was the minority in this case and the masses were afraid of going in to conquer the land that was in front of them.

Statement of fear

> But the men that went up with him said, We be not able to go up against the people; for they are stronger than we. And they brought up an evil report of the land which they had searched unto the children of Israel, saying, The land, through which we have gone to search it, is a land that eateth up the inhabitants thereof; and all the people that we saw in it are men of a great stature. And there we saw the giants, the sons of Anak, which come of the giants: and we were in our own sight as grasshoppers, and so we were in their sight.
>
> -Numbers 13:31-33

Whenever God attempts to take you into a new place, fear will always try to rob your harvest. People will see you as you see yourself. If you are not confident in your self, don't expect others to have confidence in you either. The people were self-defeated because of their own fear, and because of their perspective of themselves. If you have people around you that are constantly minimizing their destiny and losing the battle before it even begin, you may have a member of fear on your team. Where fear is, faith cannot be! We all know without faith, it is impossible to please God!

Winning begins within your perception of a matter. Boldness plays a major role on your team and in most cases it (boldness) will be the determining factor of your success. Every possession God called his people into took a level of boldness to get them into it and it also took boldness to keep it. God commanded Joshua to be strong and very courageous. Joshua obeyed the command and marched into the promise land with boldness. There is a promise land that

God is calling you and I into and it's going to take boldness to get us there.

Giants, Lions, and Bears

And David said unto Saul, Thy servant kept his father's sheep, and there came a lion, and a bear, and took a lamb out of the flock: And I went out after him, and smote him, and delivered it out of his mouth: and when he arose against me, I caught him by his beard, and smote him, and slew him.

Thy servant slew both the lion and the bear: and this uncircumcised Philistine shall be as one of them, seeing he hath defied the armies of the living God. David said moreover, The LORD that delivered me out of the paw of the lion, and out of the paw of the bear, he will deliver me out of the hand of this Philistine. And Saul said unto David, Go, and the LORD be with thee.

-1 Samuel 17:34-37

In every believer's life we will face giants, lions, and bears. Trials will present themselves to you, and try to fill your life with fear. Some of our giants are financial, some are physical, and some are spiritual and so on. Our "lions" are roaring and our "bears" are steady clawing at us but we must stand firm and refuse to allow any test to move us out of our place with our God! The bible teaches us that Satan roams around as a roaring lion seeking to devour Gods people. Satan is always seeking out a new member and he will come after us by all means necessary. If we are not careful, we will exalt, and over-inflate our trials so that they will appear to be much larger than they really are. On the other side of every test, there will be promotion!

A Giant Promotion

And he stood and cried unto the armies of Israel, and said unto them, Why are ye come out to set your battle in array? am not I a Philistine, and ye servants to Saul? choose you a man for you, and let him come down to me. If he be able to fight with me, and to kill me, then will we be your servants: but if I prevail against him, and kill him, then shall ye be our servants, and serve us. And the Philistine said, I defy the armies of Israel this day; give me a man, that we may fight together. When Saul and all Israel heard those words of the Philistine, they were dismayed, and greatly afraid.

-1 Samuel 17:8-11

And David left his carriage in the hand of the keeper of the carriage, and ran into the army, and came and saluted his brethren. And as he talked with them, behold, there came **up the** champion, the Philistine of Gath, Goliath by name, out of the armies of the Philistines, and spake according to the same words: and David heard them. And all the men of Israel, when they saw the man, fled from him, and were sore afraid. And the men of Israel said, Have ye seen this man that is come up? surely to defy Israel is he come up: and it shall be, that the man who killeth him, the king will enrich him with great riches, and will give him his daughter, and make his father's house free in Israel. And David spake to the men that stood by him, saying, What shall be done to the man that killeth this Philistine, and taketh away the reproach from Israel? for who is this uncircumcised Philistine, that he should defy the armies of the living God? And the people answered him after this manner, saying, So shall it be done to the man that killeth him.

-1 Samuel 17:22-27

The prosperity of a nation was stunted and at a stand-still because fear had gripped the hearts of the people. Promotion awaited David but he probably didn't think it was coming through defeating a giant. If you really look into the matter, it was the fear of David's brothers and the fear of the men of Israel that gave David the opportunity to fight Goliath. The victory over Goliath gave David the testimony he was in need of to be promoted. Although God probably would have promoted David some other time in his life, it wouldn't have been that time. David's boldness worked together with his brother's fear and gave him the opportunity to fight the fight he desperately needed to be ushered into the next phase of his life.

The king was ready to reward the one that defeated Goliath with riches and honor, and God had David in mind to be that man. God has your best interest at heart and you are constantly on the mind of God. There are giants in your life that God allowed to be there because he trust that you will defeat them and enter into your promotion in life. Through all of your giants in life, try to stay focused and trust in your God just as your God trust in you. You will overcome your giants and reap the benefits of your fight!

CHAPTER 4

Doubt

(Thomas and rest of disciples)

Then the LORD said, "I will surely return to you about this time next year, and Sarah your wife will have a son." Now Sarah was listening at the entrance to the tent, which was behind him. Abraham and Sarah were already old and well advanced in years, and Sarah was past the age of childbearing. So Sarah laughed to herself as she thought, "After I am worn out and my master is old, will I now have this pleasure?" Then the LORD said to Abraham, "Why did Sarah laugh and say, 'Will I really have a child, now that I am old?' Is anything too hard for the LORD? I will return to you at the appointed time next year and Sarah will have a son."

-Genesis 18:10-14

GOD HAS A WAY OF transforming those who doubt him into firm believers. The funny part about it is God will allow people to be in the midst of you that doubt you about everything you are doing. They doubt your marriage, your ministry, your faith, your abilities and your dreams. God will allow these people to hang around so that he will get the glory! In my years of pastoring, I have experienced my share of people in doubt of my ministry. There were people that came to the church just to laugh and make fun of what took place during the service. People always seem to doubt what they don't understand. Some didn't understand the gift of tongues; others didn't understand the gift of the word of knowledge or even praising God in the dance. So what else could they do but laugh like Sarah did. The only problem was, they didn't know they were next in line to operate in the same field they made fun of.

What a sense of humor our God has. Some laugh at God but God knows that he will get the last laugh. God knows how to get the glory! Although this doubting spirit can become discouraging, it is another necessity for your destiny.

Sarah was eavesdropping on a conversation between her lord (Abram), and her Lord (God). What she heard was so breathtaking, doubt found a home in her heart and she began to laugh at the thoughts God directed toward her family. We all know the outcome of her story and how God blessed her with a promised seed in the midst of her doubt. This is what God is setting up for you.

Gods' got a blessing in the midst of your doubt and in the presence of those who doubt you. He promised to prepare a table for us in the presence of our enemies. God raised up a great nation out of the loins of Sarah's doubt. Isaac was one of the more prominent leaders in the land that was birthed out in spite of doubt. God will take the doubt around you and birth out nations through you that will change the world!

Jesus immediately reached out and grabbed him. "You have so little faith," Jesus said. "Why did you doubt me?"

-Matthew 14:31

For some, doubt is the fuel that gives the individual who is being doubted the motivation to succeed. Had not God allowed someone to doubt you, you may have given up on your dream(s). I myself am a witness to this fuel. There were times I felt like giving up but I was reminded of those whom I knew doubted me. I gained the fuel I was in need of and was able to accomplish many things that I wouldn't have if it weren't for doubt. What am I trying to say? Doubt is not good, but some kind of way God will make it work for good.

Although Jesus was God in the flesh, and was able to do all things, there were still some around him who doubted. Most people try to put all the doubting on Thomas, however Jesus had many people to doubt him including one of my favorites "The Rock" (Peter). In the scripture above we see that the Lord rebuked Peter for his doubt. He rebuked Peter but yet allowed Peter to hang around. Jesus was a wise man and knew he was in need of all those that accompanied him to push him to the cross.

You may not understand it now but God will allow all those around you, be it good or evil, to push you into your dream(s). It's absolutely amazing how the hand of God moves upon situations that we see no light in, but some kind of way he brings out the best and allows us to reap the best rewards even at times doubt is found within us.

Now Thomas (called Didymus), one of the Twelve, was not with the disciples when Jesus came. So the other disciples told him, "We have seen the Lord!" But he said to them, "Unless I see the nail marks in his hands and put my finger where the nails were, and put my hand into his side, I will not believe it." A week later his disciples were in the house again, and Thomas was with them. Though the doors were locked, Jesus came and stood among them and said, "Peace be with you!" Then he said to Thomas, "Put your finger here; see my hands. Reach out your hand and put it into my side. Stop doubting and believe." Thomas said to him, "My Lord and my God!" Then Jesus told him, "Because you have seen me, you have believed; blessed are those who have not seen and yet have believed."

John 20:24-29

Doubt surrounds the best of us. I don't believe no one would raise their hand to voluntarily sign up for a company of doubters but that doesn't automatically eliminate them from around us. We are enjoying life one moment, and the next moment we find ourselves in situations we have no clue how we entered into them. One minute people are fully committed to you and the vision God has shared with you and the next minute they're not.

Have your faith ever got you in trouble. You believed so much for so long and it seemed as though what you believed was so far from manifesting that it caused you to lighten up a little on what you believed. At this particular occasion, Thomas had been through so much in his life that his trials sucked a great amount of his faith from him. At one point Thomas faith was high and full of zeal as he stated in John 11:16 …**"let us also go that we may die with him."** As time went on his faith gets a little worn and he didn't want to believe any more. Thomas is ridiculed as being a doubter but I feel that he was suffering from the disappointments of life and didn't want to be disappointed again so he made the statement in John 20:25 "…**Except I shall see in his hands the print of the nails, and put my finger into the print of the nails, and thrust my hand into his side, I will not believe."** Sometimes the disappointments in life will place your faith at a stand still as it did with Thomas. In these times you must know that God is yet on your side and he will see you through.

Keep it Moving

In the beginning until now God has never stopped moving. In Genesis 1:2 we see the word states … And the Spirit of God *moved* upon the face of the waters." In many cases in scripture, it draws us in to see that Jesus was always on the move going from town to town. Jesus also stated in John 5:17 "My father worketh hitherto, and I work." In other words Jesus longs for us to know that up until this moment God has never stopped moving.

Although doubters surrounded Jesus he didn't allow their doubt to cease the work of God. There is a temptation to quit when you have the knowledge that you are being doubted but we must continue on even through the seasons we feel challenged with doubt. Doubt is sent out by Satan with the agenda of sabotaging all God has instructed us to do. I want to stress to you that if you get the mind of Christ and keep it moving in life, there is nothing inside of your assignment you cannot accomplish. The saddest news some of us will hear is how much further we could have gone or how much more we could have accomplished if we would have just kept moving. If it were possible, when you get to heaven to see all the wealth we allowed doubt to steal from us it would shock us all. You can do it if you keep it moving!

The Deflator

And he suffered no man to follow him, save Peter, and James, and John the brother of James. And he cometh to the house of the ruler of the synagogue, and seeth the tumult, and them that wept and wailed greatly. And when he was come in, he saith unto them, Why make ye this ado, and weep? the damsel is not dead, but sleepeth. And they laughed him to scorn. But when he had put them all out, he taketh the father and the mother of the damsel, and them that were with him, and entereth in where the damsel was lying.

And he took the damsel by the hand, and said unto her, Talitha cumi; which is, being interpreted, Damsel, I say unto thee, arise. And straightway the damsel arose, and walked; for she was of the age of twelve years. And they were astonished with a great astonishment. And he charged them straitly that no man should know it; and commanded that something should be given her to eat.

-Mark 5:37-43

If you are not careful, doubt will altogether deflate what God has announced to be alive in your life. On many instances before Jesus would work a miracle he would ask, "Believe ye that I am able to do this. In this case, doubt allowed Jesus to teach two classes at one time. Class number one was the class he taught to all those he put out. Jesus taught them that doubt would not allow you to enter a lot of places in life. He taught them in order for this girl to be "inflated" everyone in the room must believe. Class number two was the class he taught to those he allowed to stay in. He taught them that although doubt is a bad thing, he showed them that he would use their doubt and turn it into a good thing by teaching all that remained in the room how to kick doubt out.

So you may have a few people that surround you with doubt. As Jesus did, you can use the doubt of others as a tool to teach others around you to always believe. Our learning is all in the way we observe a thing. Again I write in order to bring the reader into a broader perspective of life. There is victorious living awaiting you even in the midst of doubt!

More than a Conqueror

What shall we then say to these things? If God be for us, who can be against us? He that spared not his own Son, but delivered him up for us all, how shall he not with him also freely give us all things? Who shall lay any thing to the charge of God's elect? It is God that justifieth. Who is he that condemneth? It is Christ that died, yea rather, that is risen again, who is even at the right hand of God, who also maketh intercession for us.

Who shall separate us from the love of Christ? shall tribulation, or distress, or persecution, or famine, or nakedness, or peril, or sword? As it is written, For thy sake we are killed all the day long; we are accounted as sheep for the slaughter. Nay, in all these things we are more than conquerors through him that loved us.

-Romans 8:31-37

Beyond all those who will ever doubt us, it will benefit us to know that God is for us. This is very encouraging to know because the scripture goes on to say "If" God is for us, who can be against us. Although it may seem as though there are not many people that believe in you, it would surprise you to know you really have supporters and a remnant that truly believe in the vision God has planted within you. On the other hand I must tell you the truth, there are countless people that laugh you to scorn and are definite starters of doubt on your line-up. Keep in mind that no one but Jesus has ever died for you and rose again to assure you dominion on earth and a right to eternal life with your very own mansion in heaven.

There are some that I wish to encourage to remind you of the things God has allowed and empowered you to conquer. You have conquered things such as the pains of divorce, the clutches of drug and alcohol addiction, depression, cancer, and so on. If you have conquered and overcame all of what you've been through, surely you can overcome those who doubt you. Jesus died and rose again and declared that "all power" was given unto him. My friend he then invested that power within you and stained you to be more than a conqueror!

CHAPTER 5

Denial

(Peter and rest of disciples)

Then saith Jesus unto them, All ye shall be offended because of me this night: for it is written, I will smite the shepherd, and the sheep of the flock shall be scattered abroad. But after I am risen again, I will go before you into Galilee.

Peter answered and said unto him, Though all men shall be offended because of thee, yet will I never be offended.

Jesus said unto him, Verily I say unto thee, That this night, before the cock crow, thou shalt deny me thrice. Peter said unto him, Though I should die with thee, yet will I not deny thee. Likewise also said all the disciples.

-Matthew 26:31-35

Now Peter sat without in the palace: and a damsel came unto him, saying, Thou also wast with Jesus of Galilee. But he denied before them all, saying, I know not what thou sayest.

And when he was gone out into the porch, another maid saw him, and said unto them that were there, This fellow was also with Jesus of Nazareth. And again he denied with an oath, I do not know the man.

And after a while came unto him they that stood by, and said to Peter, Surely thou also art one of them; for thy speech bewrayeth thee. Then began he to curse and to swear, saying, I know not the man. And immediately the cock crew. And Peter remembered the word of Jesus, which said unto him, Before the cock crow, thou shalt deny me thrice. And he went out, and wept bitterly.

-Matthew 26:69-75

H AVE YOU EVER BEEN DENIED credit, health insurance, job promotions, or a job period? Maybe none from the above mentioned, but I'm sure you have been denied of something in life. Maybe you had a crush on someone and they denied you the chance of a date. Whatever the case may be denial leaves a bad taste in your mouth that you carry much longer than you would like to. Denial paints a stain of rejection within your spirit that only God can wash out. Although denial is painful, it is also useful. Please hear me when I say, God will use *anything* to help push your dream(s) out of you.

There were a few times in my life when I experienced being denied. God connected me with people that he allowed me to coach and mentor for a season. Whatever the reason may be, they decided they didn't want to walk in union anymore so they left. I have no problem with that, however I had a problem with them acting as if they never knew me. Not that they had to, but it was funny to see that they refused to put my name on any resume, bio, or credentials. It was total denial and at the time it didn't feel good. I didn't see God nowhere in it at first but as time passed on I saw how God used my denial for my authorization into another phase of ministry. It didn't feel good then but today I bless God for allowing this process in my life. I can see clearly now that all things certainly work together for the good!

Jesus was on his way and closer than ever to fulfilling his assignment. Peter followed him from afar off to see what would become of his leader. The heat was getting too hot for Peter but he was still trying to show support to his leader. Peter didn't know it but his denial had to happen. Jesus had an assignment and that assignment was for him only. When Jesus left the throne, his purpose was the cross and denial was an essential part of that purpose.

Family

> When my father and my mother forsake me, then the LORD will take me up.
>
> -Psalm 27:10

> A brother will betray his brother to death, a father will betray his own child, and children will rebel against their parents and cause them to be killed.
>
> -Matthew 10-21 (NLT)

As much as we love family, they are not exempt from turning their back and denying us. By any and all means necessary is Satan's motto. He will use anybody he can to try to usher discouragement your way. Satan has the knowledge to know he must use those that are close to you and that carry weight in your life. The average person off the streets that you have no connection with is least likely to steal a few nights of your sleep. Satan desires to use close friends and relatives such as our mothers and fathers. It was Joseph's father that didn't fully support his dream. David's father didn't consider him in the running for being anointed as king. Timothy's father wasn't there and he had to be raised by his mother Eunice and his grandmother Lois. Jesus knew this was the case so he already positioned himself to pick us up when our mothers and fathers forsake and deny us. Thank God for a "High Priest" who can be touched by the feelings of our infirmities!

Then Jesus told them, "A prophet is honored everywhere except in his own hometown and among his relatives and his own family.

-Mark 6:4 (NLT)

You would think those that witnessed you grow up and become the man or woman of God you have become would find it effortless to applaud your accomplishments. On the contrary it's hard to even get support from those you grew up with. In most cases God will direct you away from the familiar so your gifts and talents will be able to flourish as he intended them to. God told Abram to get out of his country and from his kindred unto a land that he (God) would show Abram.

Most of the time your greatest victories will be held outside of what and whom you are familiar with. God wants to bless you beyond measure but you have to be on alert of the familiar. Jesus was a prophet but was limited to miracles in his hometown. Denial comes from those we love most but it will launch us into our greatest accomplishments!

He came unto his own, and his own received him not.

-John 1:11

Words can never express the feeling of isolation one will experience within the depths of their heart when they are denied and rejected by their own people. Although this rejection was bad for Jesus, it was great for you and me. After this denial, Jesus opened up and said, "Whosoever will let him come". See how this denial worked in a positive way for the entire world. I thank God for pronouncing the call of *"whosoever will"*. If it wasn't for Jesus's denial there's no telling where the world would be. Just as Jesus took his denial and changed the world, God will use all the times you've been denied and cause them to work for you instead of against you! Change is all in the way you view and go through your situation.

Rejection

> And the LORD said unto Samuel, How long wilt thou mourn for Saul, seeing I have rejected him from reigning over Israel? fill thine horn with oil, and go, I will send thee to Jesse the Bethlehemite: for I have provided me a king among his sons. And Samuel said, How can I go? if Saul hear it, he will kill me. And the LORD said, Take an heifer with thee, and say, I am come to sacrifice to the LORD. And call Jesse to the sacrifice, and I will shew thee what thou shalt do: and thou shalt anoint unto me him whom I name unto thee.
>
> -1 Samuel 16:1-3

Again, Jesse made seven of his sons to pass before Samuel. And Samuel said unto Jesse, The LORD hath not chosen these. And Samuel said unto Jesse, Are here all thy children? And he said, There remaineth yet the youngest, and, behold, he keepeth the sheep. And Samuel said unto Jesse, Send and fetch him: for we will not sit down till he come hither.

And he sent, and brought him in. Now he was ruddy, and withal of a beautiful countenance, and goodly to look to. And the LORD said, Arise, anoint him: for this is he. Then Samuel took the horn of oil, and anointed him in the midst of his brethren: and the Spirit of the LORD came upon David from that day forward. So Samuel rose up, and went to Ramah.

-1 Samuel 16:10-13

Whenever we are down to nothing, God is always up to something. There was a day when God was in pursuit of a new king and Samuel's emotions were getting the best of him to the point that God had to interrupt his crying and tell him to fill his horn with oil because he (God) had found the next king. One thing we must remember is God will never allow his work to stop because of one man. There will always be a man that will count it a privilege to be used by God.

God sent the prophet Samuel to Jesse's house to anoint the next king of Israel. When Samuel arrived at the house, he had no clue who it was neither did Jesse, however Jesse thought he knew who it could be. He felt like he knew who had the potential, the physique, the style and charisma to become king! As we read we find out that Jesse's choice wasn't Gods' choice.

David was rejected by his own father and wasn't amongst those who Jesse considered for the job. David wasn't even invited into his own house when the prophet came to town. David was a reject and a mere afterthought. In the eyes of his family, David was only good enough to scoop up manure and keep the sheep from going astray. Be not dismayed my friend, God love those who are "afterthoughts" to others. You are a *"Thought"* to someone only *"After"* everyone else has been considered but God thinks about you daily.

David suffered denial by his family but acceptance from God. There are going to be times when people that are the closest to your heart will turn around and deny you an invitation to pivotal shifts in life. Understand what I have written, "people" are going to deny you these invitations but God will always come through to qualify those whom people rejected. Your rejection is going to work for you. You weren't invited to preach, you weren't invited to the wedding, and you weren't invited to the cookout or the club meeting. Yes those things can hurt but dry your tears and know that Gods' hand is upon your life and it is maneuvering you into your dream(s)!

Recovery

And she said unto her mistress, Would God my lord were with the prophet that is in Samaria! for he would *recover* him of his leprosy.

2 Kings 5:3

O LORD, by these things men live, and in all these things is the life of my spirit: so wilt thou *recover* me, and make me to live.

Isaiah 38:16

The writing of Hezekiah king of Judah, when he had been sick, and was *recovered* of his sickness:

Isaiah 38:9

Regardless of religion, race, age or ethnicity, all humankind will suffer some sort of denial and rejection in life. Denial can leave a stain on the human spirit that can cause temporary or permanent damage if we are not careful. You have to be a strong-willed individual to bounce back from some levels of denial. Always know in the midst of it all, God is able to recover you from the scars that are branded on your soul as a result of denial.

There is an anointing to heal and allow all to recover from the weighty baggage that denial leaves behind in our lives. In the above scripture, leprosy denied Naaman a clean physical body. However, God granted recovery in Naaman's physical life and gave him a clean bill of health. Just as Naaman and Hezekiah recovered, so shall you and I.

CHAPTER 6

The Sixth Man
(The Crowd)

BEING THAT WE ARE LINKING this writing as an illustration to basketball, and we have already covered the starting line-up that you need, we will now cover what the league labels to be as the sixth man. Whenever you are playing in a basketball game, it will be to your favor if you are playing on your home court. It's really important to have what the league call home court advantage, especially in the playoffs and most definitely in the championship game. The sixth man is known to be *"The Crowd"*. Once the crowd starts to cheer and get behind the home team, things begin to change real quickly. The crowd not only gets behind their team but they also get into the head of the opposing team. Momentum begins to shift in the favor of the home team. The opposing team began making mistakes by committing fouls, turning the ball over, and missing shots. In this time of the game we must give credit to where it is due. The Sixth Man (The Crowd)!

The Cheer

And the crowds that went ahead of Him and those that followed Him kept shouting, Hosanna (O be propitious, graciously inclined) to the Son of David, [the Messiah]! Blessed (praised, glorified) is He Who comes in the name of the Lord! Hosanna (O be favorably disposed) in the highest [heaven]!

-Matthew 21:9 (Amplified)

All crowds cheer. That's what they are known to do. It's not the cheering that's amazing, but rather the reason why they cheer is what's amazing. Nine times out of ten a crowd cheers because their team is winning or just made a good play. You must realize the crowd will only really support and cheer for you when you're doing well. As soon as you are not performing to the best of your ability, the crowd began to walk out. The applauding cease and the waves come to naught. Sometimes the crowd will fail to realize that you are human and every human is capable of having a bad game. I've watched it in professional sports when the crowd cheered for the "star" of the team for multiple games but booed that same player the very next game.

Jesus experienced a sixth man everywhere he went. Some crowds cheered for the loaves, others for the fish and some for the miracles. Not many had the revelation to cheer for the man (Jesus) himself. That's life, that's people! We cheer for performances and entertainment rather than cheering for life itself. People will be in your corner cheering for your preaching, your singing, and all other abilities God has given you but have absolutely no clue of who you really are. If someone haven't spent time with you to gather the knowledge of who you really are please don't get caught up in the cheer. Most crowds cheered for the performance of Jesus and the miracles he worked and not for the mantle he carried. People will cheer for Superman but walk out on Clark Kent.

The Taunt

> But Pilate answered them, saying, Will ye that I release unto you the King of the Jews? For he knew that the chief priests had delivered him for envy. But the chief priests moved the people, that he should rather release Barabbas unto them. And Pilate answered and said again unto them, What will ye then that I shall do unto him whom ye call the King of the Jews? And they cried out again, Crucify him. Then Pilate said unto them, Why, what evil hath he done? And they cried out the more exceedingly, Crucify him. And so Pilate, willing to content the people, released Barabbas unto them, and delivered Jesus, when he had scourged him, to be crucified.
>
> -Mark 15:9-15

Don't be alarmed when the same crowd that cheered for you turns around and boo you the next minute. Far too many people are losing because of their perspective of those that surround them. Sometimes our expectations of people are far too high. We expect people to act and react in the same way that we do. This is where we open up doors of opportunity for frustration to find a home in our hearts. We must know that people are very fickle and they change as fast as the weather. You could have a group of supporters one minute and the next minute that same group will be a group of critics and skeptics. Nobody on this earth will come close to being the man that Jesus was. Jesus was a man that had an agenda to do the will of his father as well as good to all humankind. For him to be cheered for one minute but taunted, mocked and booed the next, we must know we are not exempt.

The crowd turned so much against Jesus that they preferred a man they knew to be a murderer to be released and Jesus to be kept in prison. That's how society is today. We have released the spirit of murder into our homes, communities, and nations but refuse to let in the spirit of life (Jesus). Its funny how a taunt can turn into a life-long disaster. The spirit of Barabbas still roams the earth today because of the taunting of the people. This spirit is the blame for a lot of our young people chasing after the things that eventually leads to death. A crowd of people can work for you but it can also work against you. I'm talking about the "same" crowd. I have witnessed it in the local church. One minute it's "Preach Pastor", the next minute it's silence and evil looks. God longs for us to have a balance in our minds in regards to our faith in the crowd.

Conquering Offence

That ye may approve things that are excellent; that ye maybe sincere and without offence till the day of Christ.

-Philippians 1:10

No one, I repeat, *no one* is exempt from being offended by the crowd. The wisdom to conquer and overcome offence is what we need to operate in our life. Show me a man that's easily offended and I will show you a man that's lonely and friendless. We can't fall out with people every time they offend us. Satan will try to isolate you by using the crowd on a day-to-day basis to try to offend you. We have to live with people as long as we are living on this earth, so we might as well get a better strategy together on our response to offence.

The first time something goes wrong we can't continue to run and have the mentality of always thinking, "I'm out of here". How many times have you ran because of an offence only to find out the place you ran to was just as flawed as the place you ran from? So you run again and again and again only to find out you are running out of places to run. People all over the nation are leaving friendships, marriages, jobs, homes, and of course churches because they have been offended. Instead of holding their ground and allowing God to handle the matter, some find it easier to run. People have traveled the globe searching for an *offence-less* church, mate, friend, supervisor and so on. Let me save you some time searching and a lot of gas money driving around trying to find one. There are none! We all will suffer a measure of hurt and offence in our lives, but how we deal with it is very important. Divine interventions have allowed some of our lives to cross paths with the lives of others and if we are oblivious to this fact we will fall out with our God-given connection(s) as soon as the first offence occur.

The team God chooses to surround our lives with will be an offence toward us at times and trust me, you will offend them also. Do you believe your destiny is more important than your feelings? If so, sometimes you are going to have to put your feelings to the side and for the sake of destiny hold on to the connection(s) that you feel and discern to be God-sent!

Criticism

> But the Pharisees and teachers of religious law said to themselves, "Who does he think he is? That's blasphemy! Only God can forgive sins!"
>
> -Luke 5:21 (NLT)

You would think that when you turn your life around for the better that people want see you or criticize you the way they use to. I mean, now you're trying to live right, you go to church now, and you also stopped clubbing, drinking, cussing and things of that nature. It seems as though people would remember who and what you use to be and applaud you for who you have become. This is what I thought as well. Some were true supporters of my new life but there were crowds of people who I received criticism from. Although many view criticism to be a bad thing, all criticism isn't bad. There is such a thing as constructive criticism, whether the giver of the criticism meant for it to be constructive or not. The way the receiver of the criticism receives it is more important. There are some things you may be unaware of that the crowd's criticism could allow you to look into about yourself.

Jesus is the origin and central figure of Christianity and has always had skeptics in his life that did nothing but criticize his life on earth. Jesus was criticized by groups, leaders, individuals, and from some of his own people and kind. Jesus knew how to respond to or ignore his critics and also how to feed from the criticism. As we strive to follow the pattern and example that he set for us, we too should know how to build off the criticism of the crowd. Trust me when I tell you, your critics will help you preach better, sing better, live better and do everything else better that's connected with your destiny. It's all in the way you look at it! "Perspective is KEY"!

Most fans in the crowd can't even play the game of basketball but they sure know how to tell you how to play. The crowd is faithful to boo you and taunt you if you are not moving, shooting, and playing the way they think you should. We cannot stop the crowd from criticizing us but we sure can take their criticism and closely examine it to see if it's constructive. If so we could use it to help sharpen our call in the kingdom!

Weirdness

Looking into the crowd during some games you will see the weirdest people. Some paint their faces, some of the men are topless with body paint over them, some are wearing colorful wigs and others are heavily intoxicated. Believe it or not some of the weirdest people I have ever met were not in the seats of a game but in the pews and chairs of churches across the nation. I'm not questioning the salvation of some of them but I do question their mental state. Upon receiving Jesus, our spirits are saved instantly, however our mind(s) are being saved. In other words we can be saved and crazy at the same time. Some are "On" in their spirit and "Off" in their head. Our minds are going through a process of being renewed. This is why God can speak a word over our lives and instantly our spirit will catch it and receive it, however our minds will have to catch up with that word later. Paul teaches us to be transformed by the renew"ing" of our mind. The suffix "ing" means continual progress. Our minds are continually being conditioned by the word of God.

I misjudged some people God placed in my life because they seemed so weird. There were people who carried my answer as well as my wife Rachel's answer in their lives and we almost kicked those people out of our life because of their weirdness. God used some of these same people to be a blessing to us financially, spiritually, and naturally. Before you kick the weirdo out the crowd, pray to get the proper understanding of the matter. It could be that you are kicking a critical piece of the puzzle out of the box that was needed for the completion of your destiny!

CHAPTER 7

Free Agents

THEN RETURNED THEY UNTO JERUSALEM from the mount called Olivet, which is from Jerusalem a sabbath day's journey. And when they were come in, they went up into an upper room, where abode both Peter, and James, and John, and Andrew, Philip, and Thomas, Bartholomew, and Matthew, James the son of Alphaeus, and Simon Zelotes, and Judas the brother of James. These all continued with one accord in prayer and supplication, with the women, and Mary the mother of Jesus, and with his brethren.

And in those days Peter stood up in the midst of the disciples, and said, (the number of names together were about an hundred and twenty,) Men and brethren, this scripture must needs have been fulfilled, which the Holy Ghost by the mouth of David spake before concerning Judas, which was guide to them that took Jesus. For he was numbered with us, and had obtained part of this ministry.

Now this man purchased a field with the reward of iniquity; and falling headlong, he burst asunder in the midst, and all his bowels gushed out. And it was known unto all the dwellers at Jerusalem; insomuch as that field is called in their proper tongue, Aceldama, that is to say, The field of blood. For it is written in the book of

Psalms, Let his habitation be desolate, and let no man dwell therein: and his bishoprick let another take.

Wherefore of these men which have companied with us all the time that the Lord Jesus went in and out among us, Beginning from the baptism of John, unto that same day that he was taken up from us, must one be ordained to be a witness with us of his resurrection. And they appointed two, Joseph called Barsabas, who was surnamed Justus, and Matthias.

> And they prayed, and said, Thou, Lord, which knowest the hearts of all men, shew whether of these two thou hast chosen, That he may take part of this ministry and apostleship, from which Judas by transgression fell, that he might go to his own place. And they gave forth their lots; and the lot fell upon Matthias; and he was numbered with the eleven apostles.
>
> -Acts 1:12-26

Expired Contracts

By this time two contracts (assignments) had come to an end. Judas time was up from following Jesus and Matthias time was up from following the "norm". After lot casting and prayer, Gods' finger pointed at Matthias to replace the fallen Judas. One thing you must always know; everyone is not called to follow you to the end. I use to get very discouraged when I knew God allowed people to come into my life and follow for a season, only to turn around and leave the next season. Some would remain for a lengthy time, others a brief moment and I never understood why until God revealed it to me.

There is nothing in this world that is promised to be permanent but God. Sometimes if we are not careful, we can place people in the shoes of God and expect them to remain in our lives forever. I'm not telling you that there is no one that will follow you to the end, however I'm telling you don't focus on who will follow you to the end, just keep walking as Elijah did and time will tell if you have an Elisha that walked it out with you! This perspective has saved me a lot of disappointment over the years and now I see Gods' strategy in the midst of it all.

The Next Move of God

Matthias was later picked up on the team after Judas Iscariot completed his part of the assignment. God will always have someone in place to pick up where others fell off. God will never be defeated! God was doing a new thing and it was the right timing for a new teammate. Whenever we have not the slightest clue of where our support will come through in our present or future season, God already knows. Peter stated that it was time for one to be ordained to be a witness and to take part of the ministry of apostleship from which Judas had fallen. It will help you to know that God moves upon seasons. There isn't anything that remains the same but God. People change, the weather change, channels change, season's change, but Jesus Christ remains the same!

The next move of God was in place and a pair of fresh legs was chosen to carry out the plan. We go wrong when we see the legs of others are worn out and there is absolutely no more fire in their eyes and no more love in their heart for the game (ministry) nevertheless we try to keep them on the team regardless. This is a poor choice that will hurt our team instead of help it. There are times when players are hurt and they know it, but they still refuse to come out of the game. Some will hurt a ministry more than help it because of their deep-rooted tradition. Some are set in such a traditional mindset they will refuse to resign and allow a fresh mind on the deacon or usher-board. In basketball this hurts the team because they eventually get beat by a play that caused the entire team the game. They are left with regret in their spirit and a bad taste of defeat in their mind and they soon become the owner of a few bitter memories. Be attentive and on alert, you never know when the next move of God will happen in your life. Be ye also ready!

The God of Replacement

Then Daniel went to his house, and made the thing known to Hananiah, Mishael, and Azariah, his companions: That they would desire mercies of the God of heaven concerning this secret; that Daniel and his fellows should not perish with the rest of the wise men of Babylon. Then was the secret revealed unto Daniel in a night vision. Then Daniel blessed the God of heaven. Daniel answered and said, Blessed be the name of God for ever and ever: for wisdom and might are his: And he changeth the times and the seasons: he removeth kings, and setteth up kings: he giveth wisdom unto the wise, and knowledge to them that know understanding:

-Daniel 2:17-21

For promotion cometh neither from the east, nor from the west, nor from the south. But God is the judge: he putteth down one, and setteth up another.

-Psalm 75:6-7

Whenever people fall out of your life please don't assume that something is wrong with you. Sometimes you may be the cause but there are other times when people just want to leave, or God see that their time is up in being a part of your life. Sometimes we have a tendency to be hard on ourselves by thinking we were the cause of people leaving. Naomi did nothing for Orpah to leave, Hosea did nothing for Gomer to run out, and Jesus did absolutely nothing for Judas to turn his back on him. All in all, they still left!

It is God that does the replacing and he knows whom we need and when we need them in our lives. Promotion comes from the Lord and we must trust that wherever he maneuvers us to be in every season in our life, it will work for the good. I believe that whenever some people leave out of our lives, it's a sign of promotion. Instead of spending countless hours crying about it try to look at the bigger picture and see that when one leave out it only makes room for another to come in. All through the bible we witness how God always had a replacement waiting to take the place of another. Kings, family, and also friends, were amongst many categories in the bible that God had no problem with replacing and filling in gaps to keep the ball rolling and the dream going. Don't worry nor fret about the void places in your life because of those who left. Trust me, their replacement is on the way and you're going to thank God for who's coming to help carry out the work!

> And the LORD said unto Samuel, How long wilt thou mourn for Saul, seeing I have rejected him from reigning over Israel? fill thine horn with oil, and go, I will send thee to Jesse the Bethlehemite: for I have provided me a king among his sons.
>
> -1 Samuel 16:1

God is a grateful caring God, but he is also a God of production. It will be an advantage for us to know that God will never be defeated. Sounds simple but it's the simple truth. God is always ahead of us and he will never allow his work to cease because of someone walking out of your life. Have you ever seen a movie stop just because you had to leave the theater? My point exactly! It doesn't matter if you have to use the restroom, get popcorn, or make an important call, when you walk out, the movie continues to play. If anybody can stand up and walk out of your life, *let them go*! God will see to it that your movie (dream) continues.

Samuel was upset and emotional concerning Saul being rejected from being king. God made it known to Samuel that the show must go on. Mourning is a part of healing and there's nothing wrong with mourning but there is something wrong if we allow our mourning to stop our productivity. No human owns the power to stop your success just because they decide to walk out of your life. There is an ordained replacement already headed your way!

Vehicles of Exchange

As stated before, everyone that partner with you in ministry is not destined to stay forever. However, God will use some to stay long enough just to be a vehicle to usher into your life necessary people who will be fully committed to you, and the work of God. In other words, they came and left, but the exchange of who God used them to usher to you was by far greater than them leaving. They came and played their role and five was exchanged for the one. I have witnessed it time and time again in the local church that I currently pastor. Someone would join, enjoy the ministry, invite others, the people who were invited join and not long after, the one who invited the people leave.

Some may know this to be true even with basic friendship. You meet a friend and that friend brings other friends along to meet you and they really take to you. The friend that drove them into your life leaves for reasons unknown and the rest decide to stay connected. Its called an exchange, and sometimes it's the best thing that can ever happen.

The Next Assignment

And the LORD said unto Samuel, How long wilt thou mourn for Saul, seeing I have rejected him from reigning over Israel? fill thine horn with oil, and go, I will send thee to Jesse the Bethlehemite: for I have provided me a king among his sons.

Again, Jesse made seven of his sons to pass before Samuel. And Samuel said unto Jesse, The LORD hath not chosen these. And Samuel said unto Jesse, Are here all thy children? And he said, There remaineth yet the youngest, and, behold, he keepeth the sheep. And Samuel said unto Jesse, Send and fetch him: for we will not sit down till he come hither. And he sent, and brought him in. Now he was ruddy, and withal of a beautiful countenance, and goodly to look to. And the LORD said, Arise, anoint him: for this is he. Then Samuel took the horn of oil, and anointed him in the midst of his brethren: and the Spirit of the LORD came upon David from that day forward. So Samuel rose up, and went to Ramah.

-1 Samuel 16:1,10-13

There are people who have left a team and are waiting for their next assignment (team). The only thing about it is God is the only one that knows the next team they will sign with. The players may have a longing to connect with this team or that team but the final decision is left up to God. If these players (people) are assigned to your life, God will see to it that it happen for you. Remember, God has your best interest in mind. Jeremiah 29:11 "For I know the thoughts that I think toward you, saith the Lord, thoughts of peace, and not of evil, to give you an expected end."

David was a young lad that faithfully attended to his father's sheep. One day while attending the sheep, God sent the prophet Samuel to Jesse's house to sign David up for a new assignment. David had no idea that his time was up at his father's house. God was now calling the young lad to his next assignment. All of David's brothers were brought before the prophet Samuel only to be rejected.

You must be cautious and never try to force things to fit that are not ordained to be. We force ourselves into relationships, ministries, careers, and plans that are not tailored to fit our lives. In the long run we suffer the consequences for forcing our lives into tight situations. A lot of people, mostly woman has to pay a price for forcing their way into tight clothing that really doesn't fit their lives. Some of those consequences are urinary tract infections, loss of feeling in the legs, numbness and poor blood circulation.

Forcing yourself to fit where God has not placed you will soon work against you. God had the infinite knowledge to know that no one else would fit into Saul's life at this time like David would. God knew the time would come when someone would have to be anointed to play evil spirits from off of Saul's life. God also knew when the tables turned for Saul to be in pursuit of David's life, that David would not kill or touch Saul even when he had opportunity to kill that which was trying to kill him.

David's next assignment was positioning him to be anointed king over all Israel. David was a free agent and God was now signing him with another team. The young lad days of cleaning out mud from between his toes, following the sheep and scooping up manure was swiftly coming up on its expiration date. This is why it is important to be faithful where God has called you because you never know when he will call you to a greater assignment.

David was attending the sheep and wasn't even invited to his own home when the prophet came into town. Although David didn't know exactly how his life was about to turn, he fitted perfectly where God placed him. David ran for his life for a season, running from Saul, but ended up running into his destiny (kingship).

CHAPTER 8

The Bench

Philip, Andrew, Bartholomew, Simon Zelotes, Thaddeus, James
(son of Alphaeus) and the remaining Apostles that were not
mentioned as often as others.

I N THE GAME OF BASKETBALL there is a very important factor that
will take you under or help you with that extra push you need in
order to get you a championship. That factor is known to be "The
Bench".

Bench playing is very crucial to the success or failure of an
organization. It's really a funny matter because you never know
what you are going to get out of your bench players. Some games
your bench will outshine the starters and some games the bench may
not shine at all. Every head coach realizes how important his or her
bench could be.

Bench players play a lot of roles from game to game. Some games
your bench will be non-supporters, spectators and gazers. Other
games they may be your number one cheerleader and give you that
extra push you need to complete the job. In their head, some bench
players feel like they are just as good as the starters on the team and
feel like they should be a starter. If you are a pastor or a secondary

leader in the church, I'm sure you can discern when people that are not on the board or singing in the choir feel like they can out-shine someone who does have a position.

Of course Jesus had his starters, but his bench players also surrounded him. Judas the brother of James, Bartholomew, Simon Zelotes, Thaddeus, and the rest of those amongst the twelve that we have very little record about or no record at all.

Gifts and Callings

Now there are diversities of gifts, but the same Spirit. And there are differences of administrations, but the same Lord. And there are diversities of operations, but it is the same God which worketh all in all. But the manifestation of the Spirit is given to every man to profit withal. For to one is given by the Spirit the word of wisdom; to another the word of knowledge by the same Spirit; To another faith by the same Spirit; to another the gifts of healing by the same Spirit; To another the working of miracles; to another prophecy; to another discerning of spirits; to another divers kinds of tongues; to another the interpretation of tongues:

But all these worketh that one and the selfsame Spirit, dividing to every man severally as he will. For as the body is one, and hath many members, and all the members of that one body, being many, are one body: so also is Christ. For by one Spirit are we all baptized into one body, whether we be Jews or Gentiles, whether we be bond or free; and have been all made to drink into one Spirit.

For the body is not one member, but many. If the foot shall say, Because I am not the hand, I am not of the body; is it therefore not of the body? And if the ear shall say, Because I am not the eye, I am not of the body; is it therefore not of the body? If the whole body were an eye, where were the hearing?

If the whole were hearing, where were the smelling? But now hath God set the members every one of them in the body, as it hath pleased him. And if they were all one member, where were the body? But now are they many members, yet but one body. And the eye cannot say unto the hand, I have no need of thee: nor again the head to the feet, I have no need of you. Nay, much more those members of the body, which seem to be more feeble, are necessary:

And those members of the body, which we think to be less honourable, upon these we bestow more abundant honour; and our uncomely parts have more abundant comeliness. For our comely parts have no need: but God hath tempered the body together, having given more abundant honour to that part which lacked. That there should be no schism in the body; but that the members should have the same care one for another. And whether one member suffer, all the members suffer with it; or one member be honoured, all the members rejoice with it. Now ye are the body of Christ, and members in particular.

> And God hath set some in the church, first apostles, secondarily prophets, thirdly teachers, after that miracles, then gifts of healings, helps, governments, diversities of tongues. Are all apostles? are all prophets? are all teachers? are all workers of miracles? Have all the gifts of healing? do all speak with tongues? do all interpret? But covet earnestly the best gifts: and yet shew I unto you a more excellent way.
>
> -1 Corinthians 12:4-31

When we examine championship basketball teams of the past, we will see they all had the same significant factor, which we know to be a good bench! Some would call it a deep bench. If a team is going to be successful, they will have to rely on their bench play and not just their starters. As it is in basketball, so it is in your life. The people whom God has surrounding you that seems to be less significant are necessary!

Every bench player whom God choses to plant in your life will house their own unique gifts. They all have a different calling upon their life and God knows those you will personally need in your life and the diversities of gifts needed from your bench players.

Philip

> *Philip* findeth Nathanael, and saith unto him, We have found him, of whom Moses in the law, and the prophets, did write, Jesus of Nazareth, the son of Joseph. And Nathanael said unto him, Can there any good thing come out of Nazareth? Philip saith unto him, Come and see.
>
> -John 1:45-46

Here we find Philip witnessing to Nathanael about discovering Jesus of Nazareth. Moses and other prophets wrote about this same Jesus and Philip is assuring Nathanael that a good thing has sprung forth out of Nazareth. This shows the importance of our "bench players". Although Philip wasn't mentioned much, this proves to us that he supported the ministry of Jesus and ushered people to him to hear his words. There are people that will play the "Philip Role" in your life; quiet, conservative, and observes a lot but is very essential to the team.

> When Jesus then lifted up his eyes, and saw a great company come unto him, he saith unto *Philip*, Whence shall we buy bread, that these may eat? *Philip* answered him, Two hundred pennyworth of bread is not sufficient for them, that every one of them may take a little.
>
> -John 6:5-7

On this occasion we see Philip underestimating the ability of his Lord. From time to time you will have someone on your team that will challenge your authority and your ability to perform. I don't think Philip meant any harm but his response was one that said he had grown familiar with his leader and at times he allowed his fleshly mind to triumph over his faith.

Philip saith unto him, Lord, show us the Father, and it sufficeth us. Jesus saith unto him, Have I been so long time with you, and yet hast thou not known me, Philip? he that hath seen me hath seen the Father; and how sayest thou then, Show us the Father?

-John 14:8-9

Bartholomew, Andrew, Thaddeus, Simon Zelotes, James the son of Alphaeus and the remainder of the original twelve Apostles.

Below shows a brief summary of the scriptures that actually contained the names of Bartholomew, Andrew, Thaddeus, Simon Zelotes and the remainder of Jesus disciples that we don't read much about. This is not stating the lack of their role or importance to us but it raises a concern to why there isn't much information concerning their background, character, or occupations. For some of them we know what their occupation was and for others their occupation is not known. Just because we don't know much about them doesn't mean they were not of significance or less important than the others we hear more about. If they were not important or needed, Jesus would not have wasted his time to pick them after an all night prayer that preceded his choice.

Be careful not to allow the temptation to overlook someone who will be necessary for your team, but because their name is not mentioned as much as others, they are overlooked. What if Namaan's maid was overlooked because she was a maid, or the young lad with the small-bagged lunch that was responsible for feeding the five thousand? It would be to your advantage to begin praying concerning those whom God has planted around you.

> Now the names of the twelve apostles are these; The first, Simon, who is called Peter, and Andrew his brother; James the son of Zebedee, and John his brother; Philip, and Bartholomew; Thomas, and Matthew the publican; James the son of Alphaeus, and Lebbaeus, whose surname was Thaddaeus; Simon the Canaanite, and Judas Iscariot, who also betrayed him.
>
> -Matthew 10:2-4

> Simon, (whom he also named Peter,) and Andrew his brother, James and John, Philip and Bartholomew,
>
> -Luke 6:14

> And when they were come in, they went up into an upper room, where abode both Peter, and James, and John, and Andrew, Philip, and Thomas, Bartholomew, and Matthew, James the son of Alphaeus, and Simon Zelotes, and Judas the brother of James
>
> -Acts 1:13

The Mind of Others

Bench players get a chance to see the game in a different perspective. They get to view the court in its entirety and see plays that your starters cannot see. Although they are not starters they are blessed to be in the presence of the starters. They get to share their thoughts and opinions about the game and give out pointers that will be of an assist to the team. There will always be someone that can help us with his or her view of a matter. There is nothing wrong with gleaning from the mind of others. If we listen we will be amazed of what we could learn. There are no two people that have the same mind and believe me, that's a good thing! God knew we would be able to help sharpen one another with our differences far better than with our similarities. Diversity is good even when it comes to thinking. We should learn to embrace the people who God uses to bring out a different perspective in our life.

Jobs for All

In fact, some parts of the body that seem weakest and least important are actually the most necessary.

-1 Corinthians 12:22 (NLT)

Lawyers, doctors, businessmen and businesswomen that are acquainted with Wall Street are a few in this materialistic world that we live in that gets recognition and respect. Many times people who seem to be the least important and bring in the least amount of capital are constantly overlooked. What if the trash man stopped working; the barber stopped cutting, or the maid stopped cleaning. What kind of world would it be if the preachers stopped preaching; schoolteachers stopped teaching, or policemen/women, stopped patrolling our neighborhoods. I can't begin to imagine the drama and chaos this world would experience on a daily basis.

Just as people that seem to be less significant are looked over, we can blindly overlook those that follow us and surround us. It doesn't matter if certain people don't start in your life, we yet have to recognize and respect those that are bench players. The more significant parts on the human body are the parts that you never see. Internal organs such as the heart, lungs, kidneys, brain, and so on are the parts that are most important. The pastor's job is important in his church but so are the ushers, greeters, media team, and other auxiliaries as well. One man is not designed to carry the entire load. Jethro, Moses father-in-law counseled him and told him what he was trying to do by himself for the people of Israel was not good. He instructed Moses on a structure for the people to help administrate Israel to help preserve the life of Moses. Exodus 18:14-23 "And when Moses' father in law saw all that he did to the people, he said, What is this thing that thou doest to the people? why sittest thou thyself alone, and all the people stand by thee from morning unto even? And Moses said unto his father in law, Because the people come unto me to enquire of God:

When they have a matter, they come unto me; and I judge between one and another, and I do make them know the statutes of God, and his laws. And Moses' father in law said unto him, The thing that thou doest is not good. Thou wilt surely wear away, both thou, and this people that is with thee: for this thing is too heavy for thee; thou art not able to perform it thyself alone. Hearken now unto my voice, I will give thee counsel, and God shall be with thee: Be thou for the people to God-ward, that thou mayest bring the causes unto God: And thou shalt teach them ordinances and laws, and shalt shew them the way wherein they must walk, and the work that they must do.

Moreover thou shalt provide out of all the people able men, such as fear God, men of truth, hating covetousness; and place such over them, to be rulers of thousands, and rulers of hundreds, rulers of fifties, and rulers of tens: And let them judge the people at all seasons: and it shall be, that every great matter they shall bring unto thee, but every small matter they shall judge: so shall it be easier for thyself, and they shall bear the burden with thee. If thou shalt do this thing, and God command thee so, then thou shalt be able to endure, and all this people shall also go to their place in peace."

Please allow God to show you the job of those that he allow to surround you so that your life will become less stressful and preserved for such a time as this!

Seasonal Help

But of the times and the seasons, brethren, ye have no need that I write unto you.

-1 Thessalonians 5:1

For perhaps he therefore departed for a season, that thou shouldest receive him for ever;

-Philemon 1:15

Wherein ye greatly rejoice, though now for a season, if need be, ye are in heaviness through manifold temptations:

-1 Peter 1:6

Paul was addressing to the church that in the season of their life that they were in, there was no desperate need for his help. He was able to focus his attention to the desires of others that were in more need due to the season they were facing.

There are people that are in our life that are only there for a specific assignment. Sometimes in basketball, there are teams that may hire a player for the sole purpose of fouling, rebounding, shooting or blocking. Some are placed in the game for one play and then pulled out after that play is finished. Most bench players are seasonal help and are never designed to stay on your team forever. When their play is complete, God will allow them to move on.

I remember Christmas in the year of 1999. I was a car salesman and one of my customers asked if he could be a blessing to my family and financially help our family for the holidays. I quickly discerned he was a praying man and God had to put us on his heart to be a blessing to us so I said of course. I sold him the car and he gathered my information and told me that he would call me in a day or two. I have heard promises before from others that didn't come through so I wasn't counting on him to come through either. A couple of days passed and he called me to ask for my address and told me he was bringing a package by my home. When he arrived he didn't even come inside the house. He came by and handed me an envelope and said, I hope this can be a help to you and your family, God bless you. My wife and I said thank you and invited him in to join us for dinner. He threw his hand in the air, waved and said no thanks, Merry Christmas. We responded Merry Christmas and watched him walk to his car and drive off. I didn't understand until later that God has certain people he calls to your life for one specific assignment and you may never see them again in this lifetime! Some are called for the long-haul, others are called for seasonal help only. It's up to you to go to God in prayer to determine the difference between the two so you will not take offence when someone time expires in your life or ministry.

Everyone is not called to leave

In this modern day, NBA stars are leaving teams to try to hook up with other stars to win a title. This type of behavior was never witnessed in the days of old. Some stars that were drafted played with the same team throughout their entire career. Whether they won a title or not, they felt the call to remain with the team they were first called to.

Have you ever truly wondered why there were so many churches in every city but the city was yet on the top of the list in crime and poverty. Many churches in your city are divinely called. However, preachers that were never called to leave their local church have started many of these churches in your city. Just because you came through the ranks and now have the title as "Minister, Elder, Evangelist, etc. doesn't automatically give you a free ticket out of your local church. There will be some in leadership that are called to remain in place in their local church until the end. Ephesians 4:11-16 tells us "And he gave some, apostles; and some, prophets; and some, evangelists; and some, pastors and teachers; For the perfecting of the saints, for the work of the ministry, for the edifying of the body of Christ: Till we all come in the unity of the faith, and of the knowledge of the Son of God, unto a perfect man, unto the measure of the stature of the fulness of Christ: That we henceforth be no more children, tossed to and fro, and carried about with every wind of doctrine, by the sleight of men, and cunning craftiness, whereby they lie in wait to deceive; But speaking the truth in love, may grow up into him in all things, which is the head, even Christ: From whom the whole body fitly joined together and compacted by that which every joint supplieth, according to the effectual working in the measure of every part, maketh increase of the body unto the edifying of itself in love."

Here we see that many gifts are necessary in the same church in order to bring us into the unity of the faith. We must always keep in mind the word of God when we are about to make a move. Galatians 6:7 brings us into the understanding of "whatsoever a man soweth, *that* shall he also reap." For the many preachers that have turned their backs and left a bad taste in the church they left, they should have considered that the same hurt would come back to them as well.

Understanding

> Get wisdom, get understanding: forget it not; neither decline from the words of my mouth. Forsake her not, and she shall preserve thee: love her, and she shall keep thee. Wisdom is the principal thing; therefore get wisdom: and with all thy getting get understanding.
>
> -Proverbs 4:5-7

You can easily become distracted without a proper understanding of your bench players or people in your life that seems as though they are just sitting around watching the game or watching you put fort effort after effort trying to walk out the vision God has placed within you. In this world, there are no two people exactly alike. You must understand everyone is not going to think like you. We all see things differently and that proves to us the diverseness of our God.

When Rachel and I first began pastoring, some of the members that belonged to our local church constantly offended us. We were frustrated because they didn't see or do things the way we would. After many years of frustration, we finally got a revelation and an understanding that no one is going to see the vision like the leader will see it. Understanding will take you a long way in life. We now pastor with a broader perspective and a new mind-set towards the people whom God has placed in our charge.

The Coach's Call

It's the coach that makes the call on whom he or she feel is ready to come off the bench and get in the game to help assist their team to victory. Just as it is in a real game, so it is in real life. God is the head coach and it's his call on whom he will call off the bench to enter the game of life. Jesus was very careful whom he allowed to go with him whenever he was about to work a miracle. One occasion he only chose three of his starters (Peter, James and John) to remain in the room with him as he focused to awaken a little girl out of her sleep. Some of the crowd laughed at him when they heard Jesus make the comment that the girl is only sleeping. The miracle the girl was in need of was worked after he kicked them all out except for Peter, James, and John.

In some seasons of your life there will be some that God will not allow to help you. It doesn't matter if they are starters or if they are coming off of the bench. If we allow God to orchestrate our lives and make the calls, we will experience great victories in our lives time and time again. There are times that I am guilty of calling people off of the bench that I thought could get the job complete in some seasons of my life. For my wife and for myself God has opened many doors. There were some doors we included people in prematurely, and those doors ended up closing in our face. Now we have learned to pray and allow God to call whom he choose to be included in the miracle seasons God has set aside for us. He's the coach; so let him make the call!

The Bigger Picture

The minute we get the revelation to understand that it's not about us, we will be able to view the bigger picture and the reason why God allows us to go through certain circumstances. Sometimes we can go through our trials with tunnel vision and feel like God is picking on us and allowing the devil to pick on us as well. If we carefully examine scripture, every major test that someone went through was for the sake of others. Lets look closer into the scriptures below and see the bigger picture God intended for us to see.

Jesus

Looking unto Jesus the author and finisher of our faith; who for the joy that was set before him endured the cross, despising the shame, and is set down at the right hand of the throne of God. For consider him that endured such contradiction of sinners against himself, lest ye be wearied and faint in your minds.

-Hebrews 12:2-3

I am he that liveth, and was dead; and, behold, I am alive for evermore, Amen; and have the keys of hell and of death.

-Revelation 1:18 (KJV)

Wherefore he saith, When he ascended up on high, he led captivity captive, and gave gifts unto men. (Now that he ascended, what is it but that he also descended first into the lower parts of the earth? He that descended is the same also that ascended up far above all heavens, that he might fill all things.)

-Ephesians 4:8-10

Here we have one man (Jesus) who went through for the sole purpose of the world. He saw the bigger picture and he endured the cross for all of humanity. What an awesome God! Let's all remember that Jesus also descended to hell to reclaim the keys for the world. In other words, he didn't go to hell for himself but for the sake of others. It may feel like the devil has threw all of hell and everything it consists of at you but please be advised that you are going through your test to get the keys to free someone else from their despair.

Joseph

Then Joseph could not refrain himself before all them that stood by him; and he cried, Cause every man to go out from me. And there stood no man with him, while Joseph made himself known unto his brethren. And he wept aloud: and the Egyptians and the house of Pharaoh heard. And Joseph said unto his brethren, I am Joseph; doth my father yet live? And his brethren could not answer him; for they were troubled at his presence. And Joseph said unto his brethren, Come near to me, I pray you. And they came near. And he said, I am Joseph your brother, whom ye sold into Egypt.

Now therefore be not grieved, nor angry with yourselves, that ye sold me hither: for God did send me before you to preserve life. For these two years hath the famine been in the land: and yet there are five years, in the which there shall neither be earing nor harvest. And God sent me before you to preserve you a posterity in the earth, and to save your lives by a great deliverance. So now it was not you that sent me hither, but God: and he hath made me a father to Pharaoh, and lord of all his house, and a ruler throughout all the land of Egypt.

Haste ye, and go up to my father, and say unto him, Thus saith thy son Joseph, God hath made me lord of all Egypt: come down unto me, tarry not: And thou shalt dwell in the land of Goshen, and thou shalt be near unto me, thou, and thy children, and thy children's children, and thy flocks, and thy herds, and all that thou hast: And there will I nourish thee; for yet there are five years of famine; lest thou, and thy household, and all that thou hast, come to poverty.

Genesis 45:1-11

God saw a famine that would hit the land far before he even gave Joseph the dreams that he would reign. In other words, God saw a heap of people that was getting ready to perish from poverty and starvation so he used one man named Joseph to be tormented and sold into slavery by his brothers in order to save much people alive. Joseph didn't see the bigger picture until God showed it to him and his brothers didn't see it until Joseph explained it to all of them. Here we see again where one man went through for the sake of preserving many others. Its not about you, its about who will be saved through you!

Keep Dreaming

One of my most inspiring characters in the bible is Joseph. At an early age, God gave him a dream that was bound to change the world. After Joseph received the dream from God he was so excited and shared the dream with his family. There isn't anything like having great news and you have to keep it to yourself or better yet having a birthday cake but no one to share it with. Joseph loved his family so he wanted them to be involved with what God showed him. The only problem is, Joseph didn't get the response from his family that he thought he would. His father didn't understand, and his brothers hated him for his dream. The best part of the story is that Joseph kept on dreaming. The bible stated that Joseph dreamed yet another dream. You cannot allow your haters to stop you from dreaming!

It is impossible to make everybody happy so stop trying. Be the man or woman of God that he called you to be and nothing less. Joseph did not take a step down to try to please his family or make them happy. The young lad focus was to please God and God only. When your aim is to make everybody happy, you will find out sooner than you think that your aim will fall short every time. Please allow your focus to be as Joseph's and you will save yourself a lot of pain and sleepless nights.

Some players on your bench will walk with you for a while and quit when they feel like they are not getting in the game as often as they think they should. Some people just love the spotlight and when they are not shining they would rather go somewhere that will give them the stage. Many people are going to have to answer to God for leaving the church and the leaders that God handpicked for them. No matter who leave, or who remain, keep pursuing after what God has showed you and keep dreaming, as did Joseph.

APPENDIX I

Questions for Determining Your Level of Maturity in Christ

1. Do you have a dream?
2. Do you believe your dream is God-given or self-driven?
3. Do you believe your dream is for you personally or for the world?
4. How will the world benefit from your dream?
5. Do you have a slight sense of some that are called to help you birth your dream(s)?
6. How much are you willing to invest in your self?
7. How bad do you want it?
8. What are you willing to give?
9. How long are you willing to wait?
10. What are your short and long term goals that are set in place to reach your dream?
11. Have you counted up the cost?
12. Do you have a couple of back up plans?
13. Who are your examples?
14. Do you have any spiritual mentors?
15. Do you have a son/daughter spirit?
16. Do you have a teachable spirit?
17. Do you consider yourself submissive?
18. Are you loyal to your local ministry?

19. Are you faithful over what you have now?
20. Do you cause problems more than you solve them?
21. Are you easily offended?
22. Do you have a prayer life?
23. What kind of people do you continue to draw in your life?
24. Do you make a good effort to avoid drama and gossip?
25. Would you call yourself a leader or a follower?
26. Are you one that loves to debate and challenge leadership?
27. How many churches have you joined in the past three years?
28. Do you like to talk problems out or just walk away never to be seen again?
29. Do you fall-out with people when they offend you?
30. Do you find it hard to apologize?

APPENDIX II

12 Dream Killers

Gossip

Proverbs 11:13 A **gossip** betrays a confidence, but a trustworthy man keeps a secret.

Proverbs 16:28 (NIV) A perverse man stirs up dissension, and a **gossip** separates close friends.

Proverbs 17:9 (NIV) He who covers over an offense promotes love, but whoever repeats the matter separates close friends.

Proverbs 18:8 (NIV) The words of a **gossip** are like choice morsels; they go down to a man's inmost parts.

Proverbs 20:19 (NIV) A **gossip** betrays a confidence; so avoid a man who talks too much.

Pride

Pride goes before destruction, a haughty spirit before a fall. Proverbs 16:18

A man's **pride** brings him low, but a man of lowly spirit gains honor. Proverbs 29:23

Beware that thou forget not the Lord lest thine heart be lifted up, Deut. 8:11–14

Pride and arrogancy do I hate, Prov. 8:13 (Prov. 6:16–17).

The pride of thine heart hath deceived thee, Obad. 1:3

All the proud shall be stubble, Mal. 4:1

Whosoever shall exalt himself shall be abased, Matt. 23:12.
God resisteth the proud, 1 Pet. 5:5

Wrong Company

Don't be fooled by those who say such things, for "**bad company corrupts good character.**" 1 Corinthians 15:33 (NLT)

He that walketh with wise men shall be wise: but a companion of fools shall be destroyed. Proverbs 13:20(KJV)

Do not set foot on the path of the wicked or walk in the way of evil men. Avoid it, do not travel on it; turn from it and go on your way. -Proverbs 4:14-15 (NIV)

Offence

These things have I spoken unto you, that ye should not be offended. -John 16:1

Give none offence, neither to the Jews, nor to the Gentiles, nor to the church of God: -1 Corinthians 10:32

Great peace have they which love thy law: and nothing shall offend them. - Psalm 119:165

Lack of Prayer

2 Chronicles 7:14-15 (NIV)

If my people, who are called by my name, will humble themselves and pray and seek my face and turn from their wicked ways, then will I hear from heaven and will forgive their sin and will heal their land. Now my eyes will be open and my ears attentive to the prayers offered in this place.

Luke 18:1 (NIV)

Then Jesus told his disciples a parable to show them that they should always pray and not give up.

Philippians 4:6 (NIV)

Do not be anxious about anything, but in everything, by prayer and petition, with thanksgiving, present your requests to God.

Colossians 4:2 (NIV)

Devote yourselves to prayer, being watchful and thankful.

1 Thessalonians 5:16-18 (NIV)

16 Be joyful always; 17 pray continually; 18 give thanks in all circumstances, for this is God's will for you in Christ Jesus.

1 Timothy 2:1-4 (NIV)

I urge, then, first of all, that petitions, prayers, intercession and thanksgiving be made for all people for kings and all those in authority, that we may live peaceful and quiet lives in all godliness and holiness. This is good, and pleases God our Savior, who wants all people to be saved and to come to a knowledge of the truth.

Lack of Vision

"Where there is no **vision**, the people are unrestrained, But happy is he who keeps the law." Proverbs 29:18 (NASB)
"And the LORD answered me, and said, Write the **vision**, and make it plain upon tables, that he may run that readeth it. For the vision is yet for an appointed time, but at the end it shall speak, and not

lie: though it tarry, wait for it; because it will surely come, it will not tarry." Habakkuk 2:2-3 (KJV)

Fear

II Timothy 1:7) 7 For God didn't give us a spirit of fear, but of power, love, and self-control.

(Hebrews 13:6) 6 So that with good courage we say, "The Lord is my helper. I will not fear. What can man do to me?"

(John 15:7) 7 If you remain in me, and my words remain in you, you will ask whatever you desire, and it will be done for you.

(I John 4:18) 18 There is no fear in love; but perfect love casts out fear, because fear has punishment. He who fears is not made perfect in love.

(Psalms 23:4) 4 Even though I walk through the valley of the shadow of death, I will fear no evil, for you are with me. Your rod and your staff, they comfort me.

Lack of Confidence

Psalm 139:13-14 (ESV) For you formed my inward parts; you knitted me together in my mother's womb. I praise you, for I am fearfully and wonderfully made. Wonderful are your works; my soul knows it very well.

Hebrews 13:6 ESV So we can confidently say, "The Lord is my helper; I will not fear; what can man do to me?"

Psalm 138:8 ESV The Lord will fulfill his purpose for me; your steadfast love, O Lord, endures forever. Do not forsake the work of your hands.

Hebrews 10:35-36 ESV Therefore do not throw away your confidence, which has a great reward. For you have need of endurance, so that when you have done the will of God you may receive what is promised.

Philippians 1:6 ESV And I am sure of this, that he who began a good work in you will bring it to completion at the day of Jesus Christ.

Psalm 27:3 ESV Though an army encamp against me, my heart shall not fear; though war arise against me, yet I will be confident.

Lack of Faith

Matthew 17:20 NIV He replied, "Because you have so little faith. I tell you the truth, if you have faith as small as a mustard seed, you can say to this mountain, 'Move from here to there' and it will move. Nothing will be impossible for you."

2 Corinthians 5:7 NIV We live by faith, not by sight.

And one of the multitude answered and said, Master, I have brought unto thee my son, which hath a dumb spirit; And wheresoever he taketh him, he teareth him: and he foameth, and gnasheth with his teeth, and pineth away: and I spake to thy disciples that they should cast him out; and they could not. He answereth him, and saith, O faithless generation, how long shall I be with you? how long shall I suffer you? bring him unto me.

-Mark 9:17-19

But without faith it is impossible to please him: for he that cometh to God must believe that he is, and that he is a rewarder of them that diligently seek him.

-Hebrews 11:6

Laziness/Slothfulness

In the name of the Lord Jesus Christ, we command you, brothers, to keep away from every brother who is idle and who does not live according to the teaching you received from us. **(2 Thessalonians 3:6)**

If a man is lazy, the rafters sag; if his hands are idle, the house leaks. **Ecclesiastes 10:18)**

Lazy hands make a man poor, but diligent hands bring wealth. **(Proverbs 10:4)**

The fool folds his hands and ruins himself. **(Ecclesiastes 4:5)** Diligent hands will rule, but laziness ends in slave labor. **(Proverbs 12:24)**

If a man will not work, he shall not eat. **(2 Thessalonians 3:10)** A sluggard does not plow in season; so at harvest time he looks but finds nothing. **(Proverbs 20:4)**

Go to the ant, you sluggard; consider its ways and be wise! It has no commander, no overseer or ruler, yet it stores its provisions in summer and gathers its food at harvest. **(Proverbs 6:6-8)**

Procrastination

The soul of the sluggard craves and gets nothing, while the soul of the diligent is richly supplied.

Proverbs 27:1 ESV Do not boast about tomorrow, for you do not know what a day may bring.

Proverbs 12:24 ESV The hand of the diligent will rule, while the slothful will be put to forced labor.

Proverbs 20:4 ESV The sluggard does not plow in the autumn; he will seek at harvest and have nothing.

Luke 9:59-62 ESV To another he said, "Follow me." But he said, "Lord, let me first go and bury my father." And Jesus said to him, "Leave the dead to bury their own dead. But as for you, go and proclaim the kingdom of God." Yet another said, "I will follow you, Lord, but let me first say farewell to those at my home." Jesus said to him, "No one who puts his hand to the plow and looks back is fit for the kingdom of God."

Un-Forgiveness/Grudges

Bearing with one another and, if one has a complaint against another, forgiving each other; as the Lord has forgiven you, so you also must forgive.

-Colossians 3:13

For if you forgive others for their transgressions, your heavenly Father will also forgive you. But if you do not forgive others, then your Father will not forgive your transgressions.

-Matthew 6:14-15

Then Peter came and said to Him, Lord, how often shall my brother sin against me and I forgive him? Up to seven times? Jesus said to him, I do not say to you, up to seven times, but up to seventy times seven.

Matthew 18:21-

Whenever you stand praying, forgive, if you have anything against anyone, so that your Father who is in heaven will also forgive you your transgressions. But if you do not forgive, neither will your Father who is in heaven forgive your transgressions.

–Mark 11:25-26

APPENDIX III

Scriptures of Meditation as Pertaining to You, your Dream, and your Team.

Trust in the LORD with all thine heart; and lean not unto thine own understanding. In all thy ways acknowledge him, and he shall direct thy paths.

-Proverbs 3:5-6

There hath no temptation taken you but such as is common to man: but God is faithful, who will not suffer you to be tempted above that ye are able; but will with the temptation also make a way to escape, that ye may be able to bear it.

But he knoweth the way that I take: *when* he hath tried me, I shall come forth as gold.

-Job 23:10

For my thoughts are not your thoughts, neither are your ways my ways, saith the LORD. For as the heavens are higher than the earth, so are my ways higher than your ways, and my thoughts than your thoughts. For as the rain cometh down, and the snow from heaven, and returneth not thither, but watereth the earth, and maketh it bring forth and bud, that it may give seed to the sower, and bread to the eater: So shall my word be that goeth forth out of my mouth: it shall not return unto me void, but it shall accomplish that which I please, and it shall prosper in the thing whereto I sent it.

-Isaiah 55:8-11

Now unto him that is able to do exceeding abundantly above all that we ask or think, according to the power that worketh in us,

-Ephesians 3:20

Let the wicked forsake his way, and the unrighteous man his thoughts: and let him return unto the LORD, and he will have mercy upon him; and to our God, for he will abundantly pardon. For my thoughts are not your thoughts, neither are your ways my ways, saith the LORD. For as the heavens are higher than the earth, so are my ways higher than your ways, and my thoughts than your thoughts. For as the rain cometh down, and the snow from heaven, and returneth not thither, but watereth the earth, and maketh it bring forth and bud, that it may give seed to the sower, and bread to the eater: So shall my word be that goeth forth out of my mouth: it shall not return unto me void, but it shall accomplish that which I please, and it shall prosper in the thing whereto I sent it.

-Isaiah 55:7-11

And the LORD answered me, and said, Write the vision, and make it plain upon tables, that he may run that readeth it. For the vision is yet for an appointed time, but at the end it shall speak, and not lie: though it tarry, wait for it; because it will surely come, it will not tarry.

-Habakkuk 2:2-3

And they rose early in the morning, and went forth into the wilderness of Tekoa: and as they went forth, Jehoshaphat stood and said, Hear me, O Judah, and ye inhabitants of Jerusalem; Believe in the LORD your God, so shall ye be established; believe his prophets, so shall ye prosper.

-2 Chronicles 20:20

And we know that all things work together for good to them that love God, to them who are the called according to his purpose.

–Romans 8:28

For I know the thoughts that I think toward you, saith the LORD, thoughts of peace, and not of evil, to give you an expected end.

–Jeremiah 29:11

But as for you, ye thought evil against me; *but* God meant it unto good, to bring to pass, as *it is* this day, to save much people alive.

–Genesis 50:20

"AFTERWORD"

M Y GOAL FOR THIS WRITING was to bring the readers mind into a broader perspective of life and the unlimited strategy of our Sovereign God. God created mankind in his image but in return man limits God by bringing him into their image. Just because we can't understand why God allows certain things in life to occur doesn't take anything from his omniscience. I trust God that a deeper revelation has opened up to you concerning the people that he allows to surround your life on a day-to-day basis. Be it good or bad, God will see to it that the people around you will play a part in pushing you into victory and making sure your dream(s) are fulfilled.

I believe in what I call *"Emptying Out"*. I feel that everything and every gift God placed into man from the beginning of time shouldn't follow them to the grave. I believe that God longs for his creation to empty out while we are on the earth. There may be people in your life that you would have never picked yourself that God placed there to help you empty out. The bad supervisor you may have will teach you how to be a good one. The rude neighbor allows you to recognize your gift of patience and grooms your self-control. The disobedient child forces you to the altar therefore bringing you into the presence of the Lord.

Depending on the angle we are looking from, we will be able to see there is good in every situation. We can inherit good concepts out of good people as well as those we define to be not so good. There is a team that is so well put together on your behalf to force you into success! Every person that your life crosses paths with has a role in your life. Those that love you, those that are neutral towards you, as well as your haters all have a role. Through it all, keep walking and trust God and you will see that you can't lose!

ABOUT THE AUTHOR

Ronald Wilson is a native of Wilmington NC, and now currently resides in Greensboro NC. He and his wife, Rachel, are the founding pastors of New Life Worship Center of Greensboro NC. Raised only by his mother, Ronald witnessed the hand of God upon his family as God provided and carried them through many tough times. Wilson was saved in 1992 from a life of poverty, drugs and violence. Ronald ministered his initial sermon a year after receiving Christ in his life. Wilson is a husband, father, pastor and mentor to many and has a deep passion for the advancement of the Kingdom of God.

CONTACT THE AUTHOR

Ronald Wilson
803A McCormick Street
Greensboro, NC 27403
336 312 8470
336 740 5919
336 508 3504
www.nlwctoday.com

You may also contact New Life Worship Center Media Ministry
for additional ministry tools and resources from Ronald Wilson @
336 271 2838.